CHOOSING

TO

CHOOSE

BETTER

How Living More Like Jesus

Changes Everything

By Jennifer Usselman

DEDICATION

To Christ firstly, who woke me from my slumber of indifference, leading me to a better version of myself and, therefore, a much better life now and life eternal with Him.

Also, for my dear family and friends, who make my life's moments rich and inspire me to choose better. You are my every moment's muse, my heart.

TABLE OF CONTENTS

CHOOSING…

ACKNOWLEDGMENTS

I would be remiss if I did not mention those who brought me to this moment of publishing this book:

My mom, whose love runs deeper than I deserve most days and who checked this work early on for grammatical errors and wrong turns. Thank you.

My editor, Britt Clarke, who led me down the "write" path more times than I can count. Thanks for helping me make this dream come true.

Carolyn, who taught me a better way by leading me toward a real and authentic relationship with Christ and who helped give written form to my scattered thoughts. Words now fall short. Thank you.

My family. I would not be so passionate about doing better if you were not with me giving all purpose. Thank you.

Justine, my own superhero friend. Thanks for always being brave and loyal and helping me be better. What a gift you are.

And my small, beautiful tribe of girlfriends and sisters who inspire, lift, and carry me through. You know who you are. Thank you for being the buoy in the rough waters and the strong sail in the headwinds with me. And, for all of the belly laughs.

CHOOSING... A Better Way Through

Life is the continuous adjustment of internal relations to external relations.

—Herbert Spencer

I love choices. Don't you? I choose chocolate instead of vanilla, smooth over prickly, salty over sweet—no, actually I choose both of those twisted together! Choices are wonderful and somewhat mindless when we're talking about flavors or textures we prefer or styles of clothing and artwork. However, the choosing I would like to talk to you about is a kind that comes *unnaturally*. It is the intentional act of stopping before acting so you don't inflict hurt on yourself or others.

We are constantly allowing our outward actions to be driven by our fickle feelings, sometimes consciously and sometimes unconsciously, sometimes for the better and sometimes for the worse. At times it can seem we have no control. The trick is to pause in the space between, after a feeling prompts us and before choosing a potentially harmful expression or action. We must stop,

1

breathe, wait, and think just a moment. Only then can we choose rather than simply react.

I have many times (too many times) not heeded this advice and acted poorly, very un-grown-up like. In the past, I was a pro at having mom-and-wife tantrums at the expense of my family and choosing damaging words and actions. But I finally realized it was time to choose better. Grown-ups ought to grow, after all, and for me personally, it was high time I did some of that.

Choosing better for me looks like deciding to be more patient with my kids and husband when they cannot seem to do things quickly or cleanly enough for my taste. I slow down and stop, changing direction before throwing my bad attitude at them. Or, selecting kind words and encouragement instead of spewing my contentious thoughts out loud, causing arguments and hurt feelings.

It is easy to be brash if offended or frustrated by another but unnatural and difficult to choose a gentle reply that invites peace and calm while an arrow is still burning in your side. We can have agency over our responses though. In fact, for a life of true meaning and connection and one that reflects Christ, we must. It is no longer a choice really, but a mandate.

The story about Mary and Martha in the Bible has always intrigued me. It causes me to ponder the idea of choosing better and focus in on that one thing Jesus defines as better—the thing that will "not be taken away." I am a Martha-type-A through and through, so her impatience and total annoyance with Mary, her idle sister, completely resonates with me.

In the scene in Luke 10, Martha is stressed out, slaving away over hot coals to make dinner for all the guests present in her home. Meanwhile, Mary appears to be carelessly lounging and talking. Relaxing of all things! The nerve.

She is sitting at Jesus' feet, listening to Him speak without a thought to how much housework Martha is doing all alone. At last fed up, Martha snaps at Jesus, rebuking them both: "Don't you care that my sister has left me to do the work by myself? Tell her to help me!" (v. 40).

I love a good finger-pointing scene. I was getting pretty good at it myself too, before God took hold of my heart and showed me a much better way to live. Look at Jesus' response:

"Martha, Martha...You are worried and upset about many things, but few things are needed—or indeed only one. Mary has chosen what is better, and it will not be taken away from her." (vv. 41–42)

Jesus' gentle reprimand of Martha reveals that His time spent with Mary was not just typical banter and useless chatter. This was much needed connection for Mary with God Himself, something we all need more of. Jesus was asking Martha to not chide Mary's actions, but instead to look at her own to see what she could do differently to improve not only her current situation but her state going forward. Preparing food for others is wonderful and needed but preparing your heart for a life aligned with Christ and others is better. We all must remember that until we have a servant's heart like Christ, there is no real value in providing hospitality, love and serving must go hand-in-hand.

Choosing to stop the madness and learn from Christ is to correctly choose every single time. There will always be chores and stresses and worries to wrestle with in this life, but when we choose

3

better, when we connect with Jesus, we are spending our time in the most worthy way possible and we will be eternally blessed and changed. I believe that truly joy-filled lives and homes come from looking deeper and seeking God's wisdom-soaked lessons for us.

I am writing this book from, sadly, lots of experience with choosing badly and wishing I had an enormous magic eraser to just wipe those moments away and give me a clean slate instead of enough material for a book on bad and embarrassing choices. God does not allow such an easy and paltry way to change our hearts and lives, though. Instead, He uses our mistakes, hurts, and mishaps to draw us closer. He invites us, like Martha, to stop and look Him in the eyes and then into our own murky hearts so we can see our need for His inside-out cleansing and the decision we must each personally make to be changed for the better.

This book is not deep in theology or doctrine (though Scripture is a crucial thread woven throughout). Rather, it is a diary of sorts, the hanging out of my dirty and unseemly laundry. It is in a sense where the rubber met the road on my own potholed faith journey paved with poor choices and regrets. I share my story in the hope that you and I can connect through being human and flawed but wanting better, and more importantly, that you will connect on an even deeper level with the Author of all of our stories. In Christ, we are all offered a better way and each day a new start.

Until I understood that there is, indeed, a pivot-choice to make, by getting to know God through His Word, I rammed through life and wreaked some ugly havoc on the people around me. And myself, of course. We are never left out of the wreckage we create, just one more victim of our own making. My life was a knotted mess.

Then, I walked into the women's Bible study at my church one morning and started taking baby steps toward a new life, a true life. I am so grateful for my dear friend Faye, who invited me and did not stop inviting me even after three failed attempts. She asked four times before I finally, reluctantly, said, "Okay, sure, I'll do it this week."

At the time, it felt like I had just added one more thing to my overstuffed schedule. But after choosing to finally go hear the deep teachings of the wonderfully talented women's pastor and reading Scripture with others who sought a true relationship with God, I discovered this was a clear roadmap to a better, more joy-filled way for me and my family. I learned about the "fruit of the Spirit"— love, joy, peace, patience, kindness, goodness, faithfulness, gentleness, and self-control—harvested only from God's Word and remaining close to Him. It showed me my life's fruit resembled dehydrated prunes, not this abundant, ripe, sweet bounty.

I needed help.

Have you ever felt like me? Dried out and hollow? Like you're ruining the life you have been given? I promise that if you trust God and His will for your life found in His Word, you will start to become new and transform in ways you cannot fathom.

This is an invitation to all who feel deep down, or even at a surface level, that there is hope in *real* change and that if we want more connection, calm, and love in our lives it is indeed attainable, if only we choose to choose better.

We are paused at the road's fork. Are you ready to do the unnatural?

Trust me: this will only hurt a little…

CHOOSING... Generosity: A Better Offering

You give but little when you give of your possessions. It is when you give of yourself that you truly give.

—Kahlil Gibran

Recently, I got an email from my daughter's school asking, *"Can you please help us with the yearly school auction? We are still in need of a parent to organize donations for the eighth-grade class."* I had gotten this email before—actually, many times in the past, since Ashley has attended the same school since kindergarten.

I quickly decided some other parent who was probably less busy than me could handle it. Flipping through the excuses in my head, I talked myself out of it. "I run a business, help with ministry at church, and am in the middle of writing a book. No way can I do it," I thought.

Then, I heard God's voice pushing on my stubborn spirit: "Just say YES."

"I must not have heard You right, Lord. Did You see my daily planner? Here, take a quick glance. Now You understand why I could not possibly do it. Surely we now understand each other."

I waited another few hours to reply, hoping He would change His mind. Or, that the school would email me again saying, "Never mind, we found someone."

He did not. They did not.

I started typing back an answer: *Honestly, I was hoping another parent could since I'm so busy and feel a bit overwhelmed at the moment and that taking one more thing on is probably not wise. But hey, no worries. I'll figure it out and do it.* I read what I wrote and thought, "Wow, that's terrible. I'm going to make this woman feel bad about even asking me."

I erased it all and started over. *Sure thing!* I replied, faking enthusiasm.

Even though my actual emotions about taking on the responsibility were far from excitement, it sure felt better typing that than tossing my "I'm way too busy and important" excuses and ego-filled garbage all over the sender. She certainly did not deserve that. I was the one who stuffed my life way too full, not her or anyone else at the school. I was blaming the innocent, similar to how I stuff my muffin-top belly into jeans that are just a bit too tight and then blame the jeans instead of my eating choices and absolute hatred of sit-ups.

My cramped calendar was not this woman's problem, but mine. I needed to take something off my plate so I could help with a need that I had avoided for far too long. I am embarrassed to admit that though they asked every year for a parent helper for this job, I had never said yes, until now. We cannot always push to-do items on

7

the few people who somehow always handle it all, making our lives lighter but theirs more weighted down.

Churches are very familiar with the small percentage of their congregations willing to tithe, volunteer, and teach. So many people only watch church like a weekly series on Netflix rather than engage in ways that help to benefit others. Worship should be lived out daily in our interactions, through love and time offerings, not just consumed like a Sunday picnic meal, briefly enjoyed and then looked forward to a week later. We are to be taken by the sheer joy making God smile through our giving and being generous in His name, using the gifts He has given us.

Missed miracles surround us because we are not willing to step out in faith and believe that there is indeed more when we offer more. I certainly was in that camp for many years of my Christian life. Some days I sit there still. It is so much easier to just take care of me and use my time, money and energy to shop for yet another throw pillow I do not need (I may be addicted) than spend a Saturday morning packing food boxes for the local homeless shelter.

However, the more I know Jesus, the more my life is being turned upside down in the best of ways. If I want to be more like Christ that means I must decide to live over-the-top generous. For me personally, generosity needs to be so much more than tossing some money in the plate at church or handing out a few bucks to the guy holding a sign by the stoplight. That is the easy stuff, at least for me since I have been blessed with more than I need. I know for some this is the pinnacle of generosity—we each have our own journey, and I want to be sensitive to that fact. But for my two-car, white-picket-fence life, generous living means something different and demands another part of me, something that isn't found in my wallet.

I would donate money every year for the school auction and pat myself on the back, giving myself the old "Atta girl! You did your part!" pep talk. I must remember, though, that being truly generous is the stuff that intrudes a bit into my life and causes me to sacrifice, not just spend. It is intentionally doing more for others and less for me. When I spend a little time and a little money, requiring very little of me in the process, it is not being generous. It is an emaciated form of giving but falling way short of sacrifice. Sacrifice sits higher on a different dimension.

In the Gospel of Luke, there is a scene of a group of rich people piling their money high in the temple offering box. Behind them comes a poor widow who places what amounts to two pennies in. wonder if the well-to-do bystanders scoffed at the pity of it. Maybe they had a moment of feeling righteous and patting themselves on the back just like I used to, feeling like they gave more. Jesus, however, made them an example of what *not* to do. He made it clear that the widow had done worship better. She'd given everything she had left in the world out of love for God, while many had given out of their excess with plenty to spare, out of obligation and ego, not a generosity-filled heart (21:1–4).

Jesus walked the earth as the most perfect example in history of living generously. One beautiful demonstration of this is when well-intentioned, excited parents pressed in through a large crowd to have their children blessed by Him. The disciples wanted nothing to do with it. Their popular Teacher was constantly being barraged by the needy: "Heal me! Help me! Teach me! Feed me! Free me!" It never let up. Jesus' disciples wanted a break. It was too much. It was happening too often, and it was suffocating, overwhelming. Jesus was just too dang generous, and it was becoming an aggravating problem for His companions.

In this moment, Jesus taught them (and us still today) a lesson on generosity of spirit. He corrected them, displaying how we should all desire to be. "Let the children come to me," He said (Matt. 19:14). He always let the poor, the tired, the ones in need of blessing come; He never hindered or laid guilt on them.

In a separate account, when the disciples desired that another large crowd go away and get food for themselves, Jesus challenged them yet again: "They don't need to go. You give them something to eat" (Matt. 14:16, author's paraphrase).

Can't you just picture it? The disciples, exhausted and hungry too after a long day, huddled to the side after being told this and asking each other in frustration, "Can you believe this guy?"

What they may have missed in that moment is that Jesus was not trying to annoy or inconvenience them. No, instead He was handing out personal invitations to be inside of the miracle about to take place. To be participants not just bystanders. It was an open door for the disciples to enter in and be like the One they followed.

We too friends, have many, many of the same opportunities each and every day, and we will recognize them if we stay aware and stay willing to be a part of God's story. Jesus never tossed money at lepers, the blind, or the lame and just kept walking. He did exactly the opposite. He tenderly bent down, took the time, reached out, and gave generously of His Spirit, and in doing so, true change happened. Only when we decide to connect to others with Jesus' example of love and compassion will we have our hearts of stone turned soft and made open to a generosity-marked life. God wanted to test the hearts of people then and He still does today.

These days, I am asking the tough question, or maybe He is asking it of me. It is a question that makes me wince at my answer sometimes, ashamed. Am I snarky and impatient when people come to me in need or am I full of compassion like the One I claim to follow? So many times, too many, I am the former.

This evening, at the end of another long day full of meetings and errands, between which I drove for too many hours in too much traffic, I arrived home. Weary and threadbare, I walked in the door only to discover that the house was a total wreck. (Insert eye roll here.) Dinner needed making and, oh yeah, my daughter needed help with her due-the-next-morning science project. My caged, overwhelmed spirit screamed inside me: "AAAHHH!" I held it in, though, successfully preventing the screams from escaping audibly out into the room.

I might have felt some satisfaction upon reflection— "Whew! Almost blew my top. That one was a close call!"—were it not for the alternate reaction I gave, not much better. Instead of loudly lashing out, I showed a very wringed and snarled expression on my face, because I felt I *must* show my disappointment and frustration somehow. I mean, didn't I deserve to get something out of this?

I am so thankful that Scripture never mentions Jesus making a face or snapping at those in need of Him, or in other words, acting like I do sometimes. What kind of savior would that be? I'll tell you: heartbreaking and so incredibly disappointing. So…human. Jesus is not a mere human, though, and being who He is naturally, He is generous with us in countless ways. He is the image we are to reflect to the world.

We cannot accept His gifts of love, mercy, and personal attention and then hypocritically turn around and act self-centered and irritable around others especially those we are charged with leading closer to Him. If we, the proclaimed Christ followers, are not showing His character through how we treat others then who will? It is our greatest challenge and calling and it cannot be ignored or forgotten.

It is critical that we remember to offer this generous-heart way of living to those closest to us first before others. If we neglect acting like Christ to those we are closest to, then how will they be attracted to Him? At best, they will be indifferent, and at worst, they will be repelled because the person they know that is a Christian is not showing them behavior that supports their faith, nor represents the Author of it. In fact, they are showing more reasons to not bother. If I am constantly living stingy and tight, love is missing, which means God is missing and I am missing the point.

Author Shauna Neiquist, in her wonderful book *Present Over Perfect*, reminds her readers how easy it is to be generous to countless others but neglect those closest to us. Shauna is a woman in her thirties, married with kids. Like me and so many of you, she has a full calendar. As she describes it, prior to the writing of her book, her time was often spent speaking to women all over the country at various events and conferences. She gave her all in those moments, but she struggled sometimes to give that same kind of care to her own little family. Goodness, can I relate.

In her chapter "It's All Right Here," she states, "There was a moment several months ago when Aaron [her husband] was frustrated with me about something, and the kids were wild and grumpy. And these are the words I heard coming out of my own mouth: 'Everybody else likes me better than you three do.'" Reading that sentence in her book pushed at my sensitive parts. It bruised my heart and my ego because I knew it to be true for me.

She kept twisting the proverbial knife in the next paragraph: "It's easy to be liked by strangers. It's very hard to be loved and connected to the people in your home when you're always bringing them your most exhausted self and resenting the fact that the scraps you're giving them aren't cutting it."[1] Ouch. She really presses on the hard-to-hear truth, and yes, the truth indeed hurts sometimes. Direct hit.

In this delicate dance of generous living, we must remember that giving to others is important, but not at the expense of our own families and those God has given to us as our first priority. Too often, as *Present Over Perfect* so perfectly reminds, we give ourselves generously to the easy, low-hanging-fruit people and activities like those people who are easy to please and take care of with a wink and a nod and a funny quip or two at a lunch meeting. Then, with our own families, we walk in the house barely holding on to the end of our frazzled rope and expect them to not want or need even one more thing from us. We give and give to everyone else and inch down that rope all day long, until we have nothing left to offer when it's finally their turn. So unfair.

I know I have been guilty of this way too often. The television often lures me over. "It won't ask anything of me," I think to myself. "I don't have to be 'on' for it; it just needs to be on for me." It is a shallow, one-way relationship, and all too often, this one-way affair sounds pretty good.

Challenge: What can we carve out of our days that does not

fulfill our deep longings, our families' longings, and most importantly, God's desires for our moments with others? Can we see the value in true, deep, generosity-centered relationships? Are we willing to do what it takes to have them?

God has generously given us people in our lives to enjoy and abundantly love. They are worth it. We are worth it. Part of living in abundance is being generous to ourselves where it really counts. Count me in. Let's not overstuff our lives with the worthless until we have nothing left of value to give to the people in our own homes, the worthiest thing we've got down here.

We need to be generous, yes. But that starts first and foremost inside the walls of our hearts and the houses where we live. Then, when the fruit of right relationship with God and our families is ripe, sweet and abundant, we can also be generous in giving time and love away to others too. If that fruit is still bitter and green, wait a bit. Let it soften and grow. Nobody wants our tart and sour selves anyway. If we wait until ready, then our presence and offerings will be a blessing, not a bad taste left behind.

Scripture also tells us to do all things as if we are doing them just for the Lord (Col. 3:23). Jesus gave His best every single time He interacted with others. He never shortchanged people, just the opposite. Full bounty was who He was, and abundance filled all He did. For Christ's first miracle during His earthly ministry, He turned water into wine at the wedding in Cana (John 2:1–10). And not just any wine. The people at the wedding noted it was the finest and most delicious of the entire wedding feast. The bridegroom and his family would have been incredibly grateful that Jesus not only saved them from the embarrassment of the wine running out during the celebration, but also made them look good and generous towards their guests too. Jesus could have just made the same weak wine the guests expected toward the end, but that is not His nature. He only offers the best.

Again, the thought-provoking questions rise in my heart. How should I behave to offer my best too? Traffic situations quickly come to my mind. Do I need to put my foot on the gas pedal just as someone else puts on their turn signal trying to get over in my lane? Must I press on the horn because someone cut me off, most likely unknowingly? Can I give up the front-row parking spot as a random act of generous kindness rather than acting like a crazed squirrel trying to get that last nut? Um…yes, I am guilty.

Or maybe giving our best looks like giving up that seat we have claimed on the bus when a young, worn-out woman walks on with tired "Help me!" eyes and a surly toddler in tow. Any parent knows, she needs that seat way more than we do most likely.

Doing these things would not impinge on our schedules or bankbooks one bit. But they would help others out and allow them to see a bit of kindness and love from us, and in the process maybe even see a glimpse of God Himself shining through.

I have started this way of living, and you know what? It feels great. I did end up helping with the school auction, and it really was not a burden at all. In fact, I enjoyed it and got to know some parents I never would have otherwise. Turns out that days lived in generosity are wonderful and you actually do reap what you sow.

Who knew?

CHOOSING... To Trust in the Author

We cannot always trace God's hand but we can always trust God's heart.

—Charles Spurgeon

Trust can be like an insecure, wayward friend. Here today, gone tomorrow. It slips out the back door when things get tough and leaves when we least expect it, not sure if it will ever return. Sometimes, it can feel like God is just this too, a friend who is there for the most part but when times get hard is out on a long walk without His cell phone.

We can easily trust God for certain things, like the sun rising in the east and setting in the west, predictable things that time has proven over and over to be true. But what do we do when life tips over and the drowning begins and He doesn't immediately reach out a visible, tangible hand to pull us back into the boat? When we are floundering and struggling in the waves with desperate fingertips and eyes directed expectantly toward Him for help, but we do not see Him reaching back? How do we trust when we are screaming out confusion and fear-filled words like those of Jesus on the cross— "My God, WHERE are you? WHY have you left me?" but receive only a cold, silence-filled room in reply? What are we to do with that?

Two of my dear sisters-in-law have had long and hard battles with chronic pain. Surgeries, tests, medications, recoveries, and agony haunt them with each new day only bringing more of the same awful outcomes. It is impossible for those of us not suffering in ache-ridden bodies to understand how bad this really is and how hard a typical day can be.

It is super unhelpful to tell people who endure seeming life sentences of pain things like "Just trust God!" or "Hang in there! Your miracle is coming!" It is too easy, I'm afraid, for us Christians who live a very different reality to quickly hand out Bible stories like we're passing out aspirin. It is tempting to tell how Jesus healed the woman who had been bleeding for twelve years by faith alone (Mark 5:25–34) or how the man with an illness of thirty-eight years that Jesus met by the pool of Bethesda was instantly healed just because he was asked if he wanted to be well (John 5:1–9). But, we must remember that we can't promise God's same workings in anyone or in any situation. That is His alone to choose.

We wrestle with the unfair and feel uneasy with questions like: Why does God choose microwave healing for some and slow-cooker for others? Or even no visible healing here on earth at all? It is impossible to know but reaching into Scripture gives us nuggets of understanding. Not complete knowledge, but a sufficient amount based on who God is and has always been.

Merriam-Webster defines trust as "assured reliance on the character, ability, strength, or truth of someone or something and one in which confidence is placed."[2] We cannot trust that all difficulty and pain will end or be fixed down here, but we certainly have the ability to know the One worthy of trust in spite of it all.

This is why reading the Bible and learning its lessons and God's heart toward us is critical for trust, even through the fog of misunderstanding we stand in sometimes. God has countless examples of His trustworthiness and sacred assurances written out in black and white for us. We just need to decide to get to know Him and understand that things still can appear murky, even amid the miracles. Here are some examples:

Moses pleaded for help with food and water for millions of Israelites in the desert, and God provided manna and quail from heaven. Even so, the multitude complained (Exod. 16).

Hannah was long-suffering in waiting for a child. God provided Samuel, her beloved son, whom she would release back within just a few years to live with Eli the priest and outside of her motherly arms. She had to trust in God's plans and not cling to her own (1 Sam. 1).

David begged for safety and God provided protection and kingship, but not until after he was tormented with fear and full of feelings of abandonment, as he displays in the words of Psalm 13.

Peter desperately needed forgiveness and purpose after denying Jesus (John 18:15–27). God provided both as Peter surrendered to His plan and used his life in ways that shook his sense of safety to the core (21:18–19) but changed the world's story forever.

These accounts tell us that true trust is a hard-won lesson taught through the rocky, uneven, and mysterious terrain, not by walking the smooth and easy, well-known road.

Scripture proves through very real, damaged, and needy people like you and I how God can be trusted to care for, provide for, and protect people in noticeably big ways. But not always in ways we would choose if asked our opinion on the matter. Not one of the people I just mentioned in Scripture lived a life completely free of troubles or pain or confusion by God's chosen way to answer them. Thankfully though, God is not offended by our misgivings and shaking fists but stays with us, guiding and leading. God's solutions are not always clear-cut and comfortable. Indeed, often they are not. But He is certainly still worthy of our trust.

Understanding what trust is also tells us what it is not. It is not putting our precious faith in something that has failed us multiple times. Say, for example, my ability to run at a not-totally-embarrassing clip for more than two minutes. I want to trust that my lungs will not heave and flare like they are a building on fire, but alas, they do every single time I attempt this activity. I want to be one of those women who can say things like, "Sorry I missed your call. I was on a run," but no, my lungs have proven totally untrustworthy time and time again.

I also have had people in my life who have proven the same, not worth the faith I give out, sure to burn my trusting, outreached heart. I had a friend one time who was very consistent in one thing; letting me down. I would strive and do more and more for her. I was always reliable and ready to help. But all she was for me was a barnacle on my boat, chipping the paint and leaving me with scars and damage to repair. After years of this sad and predictable routine, I finally got out of the boat and learned to put my trust in better, more reliable people and things.

This life is brim-full of minor and major disappointments and joy-chipping barnacles — those things and people and circumstances that only suck the energy from us and give nothing in return. But trust is still a worthy cause. Living by faith and not by sight means that no matter the situation, we can rise above it because we trust in the One who authors it for reasons we cannot yet understand.

We may think we have it all figured out, but then the storyline changes, twists completely upside down, leaving us shocked at the events like a great mystery thriller. "What?! The sweet, young schoolteacher is the murderer! No way! I thought it was the mean, crotchety old gardener this whole time!" When this happens, we must accept that sometimes only the last page of the book reveals the purpose for the messy moments that our minds cannot thread together neatly. But we can certainly trust that the Writer will use the frustration, pain, and confusion of the story to bring its intricately woven conclusion into view and clarity. It is the "aha!" that comes after we read the last line and think to ourselves, shaking our heads, "Yes, of course!"

Mary and Martha experienced that kind of shocking plot twist. The eleventh chapter in the Gospel of John tells how their brother Lazarus fell gravely ill and Jesus, whom these siblings had come to trust in completely, was nowhere to be found. A panicked message was sent out to tell Him that His beloved friend was sick and near death and to please, please hurry. Lazarus' family was certain if Jesus were there, He would take care of him and all would be well. Jesus was a local celebrity known for healing after all; and Lazarus was not just another beggar in need, he was a close friend and confidant.

However, we are horrified to read that Jesus hears this awful news and does not go bounding fast out the door like a superhero determined to save the day. Instead, He waits. And in the agonized waiting, Lazarus dies. Jesus does not heed the cries of His friends in their direst moment; He stays put, shaking their trust and their faith. This shakes my faith some too, and my good-friend sensibilities to the core. "Jesus, this is just not okay! These are Your friends! How could You not run to help in any way You could?"

How? Because God had a glorious plan that nobody could have predicted. Jesus first wept with them as their dear friend, and then, as their Lord, He commanded their dead brother to return to life: "Lazarus, come out!" (v. 43). Death was defeated through His mercy and boundless love. This showed that they could still trust Him, and there was certainly joy to be had; it just looked different and took a bit longer than they expected it would. Sometimes tragedy is used for good that we cannot see at the beginning or in the turbulent, untidy middle. And sometimes we will not see the good until we are on the other side of this life completely.

Putting trust in God's complete sovereignty is tough sometimes. It involves not just the beautiful and fun parts of life but also the worst parts with the very worst outcomes.

God reminds me to ask myself as I read this account of Lazarus, is Jesus only just a friend I expect to follow my checklist of dos and don'ts or else I will write off? Or is He my Lord of all? If the answer is the latter, then I must decide to accept His will and trust in it no matter the cost to me and my vision of a satisfactory ending. If He is glorified in it, that is enough.

It still presses on my weak, fickle heart, though. The word *all* is a tough one to swallow, right? It feels sort of like a hard candy in my spirit, big enough that it slips down the throat and gets stuck partway. It chokes me a bit and hurts some, difficult to accept.

When I was finally getting to know God on a deeper level, I began to reach down into truth and study Him through His own words. I was not willing to accept the stories in the Bible just because someone told me they were true—I am too hard-headed for that. No, I needed to see for myself. And so, I did. I burrowed down into the historicity of the Bible and came to understand that it is like no other book in the world. Forty different authors, mostly unknown to each other and separated by many centuries and miles, wrote the sixty-six books that, when placed together, comprise a perfectly told story of God and how He redeems us. From start to finish the theme is the same: Jesus, the Savior, is the secret of God revealed to His creation.

Some people immediately choose to believe it is all a myth, but this just cannot be true. Myths are made up of theatrical depictions of gods and goddesses who hang out together in the clouds in the heavenly realms causing unnecessary drama and throwing lots of tantrums. They're like immortal soap operas in the sky. The Bible though, is written as a record of historical facts and stories including eyewitness testimony and genealogies, sometimes in such detail your eyes roll back in boredom as you try to read through it all (the book of Numbers, anyone?) The stories of Greek gods are vague and impersonal and lofty, painted with a large, fantastical brush. The stories of the Bible are full of specific descriptions of places, dates, people, and landmarks and very personal accounts set upon intricate contexts. No, this text is certainly not myth. Far from it. It is miraculous.

During my study of the Bible, I experienced a sense of awe at God's miracles of healing that occur over and over in this very special book and confessed complete trust in His caring nature and abilities and true love for each person. Soon after though, I was taught a real-life lesson about God and His character traits that never change, which reshaped my understanding of complete trust.

One day, a dear family friend called me with strained urgency in her voice, to ask me to pray for miraculous healing for her ex-husband who was not a believer in Christ and who was dying of cancer. I got right to it, fervently praying "Lord, I know You love him too and want full healing for him. Please God, give him a complete healing miracle that You are more than capable of! Amen." I was just certain my prayer would work. I fully believed what I had read earlier in James 5:15–16: "And the prayer that is said with faith will make the sick person well; the Lord will raise them up...When a believing person prays, great things happen" (NCV). I prayed and then looked forward to hearing the news of his unbelievable, miraculous turnaround. I knew God was capable. Now, I just had to wait.

I answered a call a few days later to hear her tell me that he had passed away. My first dazed thoughts were "What? God, what happened? I thought if You loved us—and I truly believe You do— that You would have saved him." Just like the sisters of Lazarus, a chilled wind of doubt sliced through my faith, splitting it open. My heart sank.

My friend went on to tell me however, much to my surprise, that he had accepted Christ just before he passed away. My heart then rose back up and just about stopped. I offered right then prayers of gratitude to the God who saves and comforts us even in death. Within the tragedy and disappointment of it, full healing still happened, and not in a temporal, quick-fix sense, but in an eternal one.

You see, sometimes the answer comes from a direction we do not expect, but God knows what He is doing. What looks like a major defeat on this side can be divine intervention on the other. We only need to look at the horror and shock of Jesus on the cross and the crazy, glorious outcome three days later to see the most acute example of this!

I learned a lot that day about God's character and about my own. I needed to not be prideful in thoughts along the lines of "My prayers are going to save the day," but rather give all glory and trust to the only One who deserves it. And be grateful for His will being done, even if it stung some in the process. His ways certainly are bigger and much more trustworthy, and we will see that if we are willing to surrender our preconceived notions of who He should be and how He should aide us in our circumstances.

"Trust in the Lord with all your heart, and do not lean on your own understanding," Proverbs 3:5 says. There is that word *all* again. God asks us to trust completely, fully, over everything, not partway, with one foot in and one foot out.

This verse also reminds us that our own understanding is oftentimes just a *misunderstanding* of His plan. In this life we stew in confusion over why what we observe seems inconsistent with what we know of God. We struggle with why some are healed and given more time while others are not, especially when we read things in the Bible like; "Therefore I tell you, whatever you ask in prayer, believe that you have received it, and it will be yours" (Mark 11:24).

But in my case, it turns out, I misunderstood God's hand in my

24

friend's ex-husband's passing. I initially thought I was not heard or was ignored when I asked for healing, but in reality, I was not only heard, but I was told, "Yes, fully and unabashedly, yes. I *will* fully heal him. Your prayer has been answered." Plot twist! Again, we do not see the last page while in the middle of the book, but He does. We can rely on the Author because He has it figured out. It is our job to keep engaging, not giving up and throwing down the book, and walking away when we don't agree with the storyline.

If trust means to rely on "the character, ability, strength, or truth of someone," then trusting God means we have someone worthy and time proven. My two dear sisters have taught me this lesson in the way they live through their daily struggle, still holding trust in God raised high like a guiding torch, even on their worst days and inside the dark, merciless nights. If they can keep going and choosing better through the bitter, then I certainly can too.

Friends, let's keep turning the pages of this crazy mystery we are here participating in, anticipating all that great stories involve: Wonder, pain, joy, conflict, adventure, and unbelievable endings.

This life is a good read, and God is the very best of authors.

CHOOSING... Joy's Deep Dive

All human joys are swift of wing,

For heaven doth so allot it;

That when you get an easy thing,

You find you haven't got it.

—Eugene Field, "Ways of Life"

Psalm 118:24 reads, "This is the day that the LORD has made; let us rejoice and be glad in it" (ESV). This verse was penned to announce God's future revelation of His precious secret: that His coming Son was indeed the One to redeem the long-suffering and waiting, anxious world. The day had come! Rejoice! When I read it now it is a reminder for me as I awaken each day to be grateful for God's wonderful plan then and now.

I should decide to choose joy for my day ahead even before I put a reluctant and unconvinced foot to the floor. It exhorts my wavering heart to say to God, "No matter what this day holds I will be glad for it, because You chose that the sun should rise to usher it in." It is the reminding nudge to my stubborn mind that encourages it to surrender over the day at hand to joy regardless of my circumstances. Can you think of anything that beckons the phrase "easier said than done" more than this?

Today, I woke up in the ache and fuzz of a bad cold accompanied by a sore throat—raw, dry, and painful. *Oh joy*. It is super hard, seemingly impossible even, to choose to be glad about such things, especially since this is not my first ride on the sickness Ferris wheel of late. I know I am in for a hard day and likely a hard few days of my nose and most of my brain feeling like they are stuffed full of cotton balls and every swallow feeling like I am gulping down sharp quills of a porcupine. I am not looking forward to doing anything at all today, actually, and just getting out of bed seems like cruel and unusual punishment. But I am called to rejoice in it? Come on.

Thankfully, I can still see through the fog of my clogged mind enough to notice a distinction of terms; that rejoicing *in* something and rejoicing *for* something are entirely different. I am not called to throw a welcome party for this sore throat (and good thing!); however, I can still be thankful and rejoice that getting out of bed is an option for me. At least my body still functions and my mind still thinks clearly—well, for the most part.

Joy, I am finding, is a much deeper treasure hidden somewhat from view beneath what is sitting on the surface of life. To find it, we must sometimes burrow down through the gritty, toughened outer layer. It is akin to digging for clams. You must keep going,

27

keep seeking, and it takes time and toiling along with some grunting effort and perhaps even some disappointment. But joy comes in the staying and finding the hidden clam. And then, going deeper yet, prying it open and discovering a precious pearl within.

It is so precious in fact many do not find it. Many of us do not want to put forth the work it takes and instead accept happy feelings as joy's cheap substitute. Happiness is nice, do not take me wrong, just not as good as it gets. Happiness is basic needs being met. I am happy there is food in the refrigerator and a bed to sleep in, happy there are sunny days I get to wear flip-flops and drink lemonade. Something, however, rumbles beneath all of that: our deepest need and aching for joy.

Jesus is this joy, friends! When we choose Him, we choose to invite in joy. Choosing better means getting to a deeper level in all things. Relationships, work life, and daily experiences are so much richer if we refuse to stop at the intersection of "happy" and "good enough", continuing onto where joy intersects our soul.

So many of us give up before we find the real treasure. We get so close to greatness but turn around before reaching the summit because we are tired or bored or weak or frustrated. But what would happen if we pressed on a bit further, even with blistered feet? What does that look like?

For me, it means saying things that need saying and listening to hard truths I need to hear about myself. It is sitting in the struggle of difficult conversations before packing it in and giving up. It is going rounds and rounds with my husband until a resolution is met and both of us feel heard and validated, if a bit exhausted. For me, the easiest thing to do is to slam the door shut on the conversation, walking out of the room, leaving issues unresolved and my heart unsettled. Much more difficult is it to stay and fight fair finding much-needed peace.

It is in such moments, when the path is somewhat treacherous, that I need to remember that after exerting the greater effort I get the greater reward. In the digging and going further, I find the glimmering joy: Relationship restored, with the people in my life and, more importantly, with my God and Redeemer. Joy is deeper than a feeling; it is a sacred place, where God resides. It is where we should all strive to live out our days.

I am reading the Bible daily, and I just finished the book of Exodus. Coming away, I am inspired by the relentless endurance of the Israelites through years of slavery, parched desert–dwelling, and more. They did not do these things happily—they were bone-tired and frustrated—but they seemed to dig deep when they needed to, often thanks to Moses' perseverance toward the reward even amidst the trials and agony of it all. He kept pressing on, exhorting them, "The Promised Land is coming! Just wait! Hang in there! Stay with me now!"

Like the Israelites, I find that too often I focus on temporary problems and not God's eternal promises. Today, waking in the bodily state I am in, I was really hoping for a light-hearted passage of Scripture to read since I feel empty and drained like a squeezed-dry orange. Well, that did not happen. I turned the page and found myself in Leviticus. And, to make matters worse, I came to chapter four, entitled "The Sin Offering." My eyes and spirit rolled back. "Oh joy, again." I said a quick prayer of minor lament, asking God to get me through it, then started my reluctant reading of the weighted words.

Heavy in its subject matter, this chapter details the sacrifice of animals; it is death and gore in its rawest sense. You can almost smell the scene, hear the cacophony of the bleating, and envision the blood offering pouring out against stone. "Awful," I think to myself. "Where is the joy in that? Lord, please tell me."

It was revealed to me in my spirit as soon as I posed the question: The joy in the sin offering is the opportunity it presents. God made a way back to Himself! He lit the path for the lost people then and for us still today to our most treasured place, His presence.

There is joy to be found, if we dig, ask, seek, and receive. Blood was required, yes, horrible. But such a blessing for the world was the last and final blood sacrifice offered in the flawless lamb of Jesus. His pure blood was the final payment; no other blood would do. No more payment required. That, my friends, is the most upside-down transaction in the history of the world. We made the debt, He paid it. All clear. Oh, the JOY!

The Greek word for joy is *chará*. Strong's Concordance defines it as "the awareness (of God's) grace, favor; joy ('grace recognized')."[3] *Grace recognized*. Isn't that beautiful? Our being full of joy is not based on us at all but on knowing and recognizing Him, the source of joy itself!

The Apostle Paul is a wonderful example for us of living a life of joy no matter the situation. His constant companion was God's grace. He was beaten, stoned, and put in prison on multiple occasions during his ministry, so if anyone in history had a reason to complain, it was him. Instead, though, this persevering faith-race runner shows us time and time again that joy is not dependent on anything outward or on anyone's own doing but on alignment with Christ in all things, even in death, especially in death:

30

"But I will rejoice even if I lose my life, pouring it out like a liquid offering to God, just like your faithful service is an offering to God. And I want all of you to share that joy. Yes, you should rejoice, and I will share your joy." (Phil. 2:17–18 NLT)

Paul reminds us that because of our kinship with Jesus, we can have joy and rejoice in it, even in the deepest darkness we experience during our temporary lives here. Christ alone contains the balm our bruised and thirsty hearts cry out for.

Because of Christ, separation from our Creator is eliminated and death no longer stings us in a permanent way. Even in the very worst of events, the horror of the cross, there is joy to be found. A quote I love is, "I can see there are good things that only suffering can bring." The author is unknown, but this is a profound truth we all should think deeply on. After the blistering journey's climb comes rest and the prize of the summit's longed-for views. After the sacrifice, the miracle of full forgiveness and resurrection arises. Joy for the world is Christ. Joy for our individual hearts is Christ too.

Wood, nails, hands. Jesus, a carpenter by trade, used these and made chairs, tables, and the like for people of His time. I bet He found joy in helping make others' lives easier and more complete. That was just His way.

Wood, nails, hands, and a crucifixion cross. The same elements used in the vocation of His youth, but now for the purpose of completing the final sin offering and His passion and mission and completing us in the process. The Apostle Paul wrote,

Let us keep our eyes fixed on Jesus, on whom our faith depends from beginning to end. He did not give up because of the cross! On the contrary, because of the joy that was waiting for him, he thought nothing of the disgrace of dying on the cross, and he is now seated at the right side of God's throne. (Heb. 12:2 GNT)

Joy certainly is worth the effort, and sometimes it takes time to find. Way deeper and infinitely more important than happiness, it is dependent on God alone; we cannot find it absent of the One who abides in it. A new car, a great outfit, a delicious meal or a vacation week away will not do it—not even close. No, joy is far beyond this temporal cheer; it is eternal and rooted in our spirit, only found in connection with Christ.

So, friend, join me and get out your spiritual pickaxe, your sharpest spade. Dig, seek, find, no matter how long it takes. Some things are too precious to leave buried. I will choose to find joy today, and I thank God that He made a way to attain it no matter the circumstance and that He pushed through the agony of the cross so He could offer it to you and me with open and love-scarred hands. Now that is something worth rejoicing in each and every day, sore throat or not, right out of the gate, no matter what the day might bring!

Can I get an "Amen?"

CHOOSING... Peace Over Pace

Thou hast made us for thyself, O Lord, and our heart is restless until it finds its rest in thee.

—Saint Augustine

Peace. When we hear the word, we might tend to think about the absence of conflict or noise. But peace does not only have to do with what is happening, or what is not happening, around us, it is also about finding a profound internal rest for our spinning souls. We rarely let ourselves just be. Be present. Be quiet.

"Be still, and know that I am God," the Father gently reminds us (Psa. 46:10), pulling us back to center. This is wonderful and reassuring to read on the printed page in my Bible but so hard to actualize in the nuts and bolts of real life while the gears are grinding and overheating.

A big part of my problem is, I fully admit, I am a multi-tasking crazy person. I am always in high gear it seems, making it work, making it better. Many days I feel like I am barely managing the moving parts of my life, like a plate spinner at the circus. "Don't let one drop…don't let one drop." I even routinely begin lifting my next thought up before my mind is placing down the first one. I must stay ahead of the next spin, so the plates do not come crashing down all around me.

So, telling me to just "be still" is like telling a four-year-old boy to meditate in the downward dog position for ten minutes—no talking, no moving, no goofing off. Such complete stillness is excruciatingly hard, practically impossible, for a young boy itching to jump and wiggle, and it turns out the same for me, a middle-aged woman with an overfilled agenda and too much coffee in her system.

Many of us have been programmed not to see the need for stillness. It is super unproductive after all. Free time in the schedule feels wrong and sad, like seeing a kid on the playground all alone at school with nobody playing with him. "Oh, poor dear, nothing to do and nobody to do it with." So we fill up those empty, lonely slots with more and more things to do and more and more people to see. We are not going to be that poor kid. Nope. Not me. No way.

There is always a new deadline at work to meet, an activity scheduled in for the kids, and that midweek evening book club meeting you are hosting at your house (why did I join that again?). I am expected to make my famous chocolate cake to serve tonight, and I still have not read the last two chapters, let alone cleaned the nasty toothpaste-splattered bathroom mirror. "Hurry up! Spin! Move!"

The words "be still" are the last on the priority list and are certainly not written in on the calendar. Being truly still requires that we let our busy bodies and overtime minds take an extended vacation. A full-fledged, no-checking-emails-allowed vacation. I do not mean get on a plane to a sandy beach in Belize (though that sounds *really* awesome); rather, this is about making room in each day for preplanned, elongated portions of rest to regroup and regenerate, time to be still. We must be intentional about filling up with the fuel that only peace and actual inner quiet can offer us. Our families and our very souls starve for it. I know mine do.

What I must remember is that peace in my home is more vital than pace. Choosing the accelerated life drains the joy and sweetness from our moments and the very health from our bodies. Our kids are suffering. Our marriages are suffering. Our deepest parts are withering and dying because we are neglecting to water and feed them with the life-giving communion we were created for, deep connection with God and each other. This only comes by taking the time required to actually honor our need for rest. As my friend Sarah, who is a life coach, says, "We must nurture all of the worthy pieces of our lives." Rest, is indeed a very worthy and often very much neglected piece of our daily-moments pattern. Breakneck speed cannot supersede the nurturing of our need for pause if we want our lives to be truly fulfilled, not just full.

In the beginning, God kept busy and mind-blowingly creative; for six days. Then, you guessed it, He rested. He designed a day specifically for repose. This was not an accident; nothing God does is. Rest was intentionally placed into His instructions to us as a part of His pattern for the best way to live a good and fulfilled life. It was a gift made just for us. After all, God never sleeps. He did not create rest for Himself.

In Mark 2:27, Jesus says, "The Sabbath was made for man, not man for the Sabbath." This truth is as important for us today as it was for very first humans created, maybe even more so since we are so far removed from our original design in our high-speed and productivity-driven world.

I visited our local Japanese garden one beautiful spring day recently and it struck me how it was so intentionally fashioned to evoke the concept of peace and stillness. The expansive gardens and tea house are clean and pure in design, totally void of unneeded adornments, and thankfully so, as they would stand out like a mustache on a beauty queen. Quiet itself, it seems, is woven into the simple tapestry of the surroundings. When you are there, you are freed to be, well…free. Free from busy and hectic and manic. It is an irresistible invitation for your soul to be quiet. You cannot help but say yes to the beckoning.

Japanese houses and gardens have a transition that is intentionally incorporated from the outside space of the home to the interior rooms. Stepping stones and rocks are placed in just the right way with enough ma (the Japanese word for the distance between, pause, or space) so that the person on the path must slow down and pay attention to their placement as they walk towards the front door, lest they trip and fall. The margin placed between the outside and inside of a home is designed to slow down not only the feet but the mind as well. Even your heart rate calms as you understand you are entering into the home (peace) and leaving the outside world (chaos). It is a beautiful way of living, a sacred way of living.

It is even noticeable in conversation between persons of traditional Japanese culture and American culture. Americans tend to fill in every gap with word noise. Me: guilty often. The Japanese, though, generally embrace and even enjoy the space, or ma, between words, and we may confound them with our need to pad any small pauses with unnecessary and frivolous ums, ahs, and likes. Our tendency toward busyness spills over even into our conversational style.

To experience sacred stillness, we must understand our need for pure, unadorned connection to God, to Jesus, the Prince of Peace. It is like Saint Augustine famously concluded: "Thou hast made us for thyself, O Lord, and our heart is restless until it finds its rest in thee." Since we were made for relationship with God, until He, the embodiment of peace, abides in us, true peace will not be present. Instead, our souls will ever be searching in vain for that missing link that just always seems to allude, like that last puzzle piece hiding deep in the crevice of the sofa cushions, taunting us until we find it and complete the picture. Once we choose peace and to live within its holy walls, filling our calendars with too many extra things to do somehow no longer feels right. It starts feeling like useless clutter we don't really want, like a stuffed closet in need of a clean-out.

Our connection with God is everything, and prayer is our way to speak to peace itself. In prayer, we stop, we listen, and we rest in the arms of the One who knows us inside and out. When we choose to pause—to link up with our true Center through stillness and quietness in Him—then we can feel whole. Nothing else is required. Nothing else is needed. Completeness achieved. We are in the sacred and holy space between.

Jesus gives us permission and asks us to come lay our burdens at His feet. He will never take peace away but only offer it freely and generously for our lives:

"Come to me, all you who are weary and burdened, and I will give you rest. Take my yoke upon you and learn from me, for I am gentle and humble in heart, and you will find rest for your souls. For my yoke is easy and my burden is light." (Matt. 11:28–30)

We can melt into the beauty of this gift and the truth that sets us free at last, and only then find true stillness.

Let's make space for space. Let's choose to make intentional time for prayer and connection to God, to allow peace to fill us rather than pace. Plates can drop to the ground. And you know what? All is still well.

In fact, it is better than ever.

CHOOSING... Self-Control and God's Best

*I count him braver who overcomes his desires than him
who conquers his enemies; for the hardest victory is over
self.*

—Aristotle

You have heard the statement "You are what you eat," right?
Well, luckily for me, that is only a figure of speech, or I would have
turned into a large, greasy French fry dipped in ketchup a long time
ago. French fries are my weakness...one of my many weaknesses,
actually. I hold them up in my fingers and loudly proclaim the
words of that seventies song: "If loving you is wrong, I don't want
to be right!"[5] I eagerly eat them all, receiving satisfaction held only
briefly before in seeps the regret, over having been once again
unable to resist and realizing that my time spent in exercise that
morning was pretty much made to no effect. Ugh!

There is so much out there to tempt us. If you struggle with
temptation way too often, with too many things, you are in very

39

good company. This is a common issue of being a member of humanity.

If it makes you feel any better, being tempted and the need to control desires comes from our earliest moments. It is in our DNA, our genes. Eve in the garden of Eden was given the immeasurable gift of perfection all around her. She lived in an environment created specifically for her and her husband. Her wants, needs, and pure enjoyment were taken into very personal and deep account by her Creator. Just think of that for a moment—amazing, generous love. The one thing missing was a cute wardrobe and shoes to match. Oops! Just one more of my own weaknesses exposed... Let's keep going.

Eve's surroundings were not only abundant and extravagant; they were also created with important limitations for her own good. The tree of the knowledge of good and evil was the only thing out of bounds to consume, the one thing with which God asked them to have self-control.

However, even with all the wonderful and perfect offerings around her, she still coveted to take something for herself from what God held back for Himself alone (Gen. 2:16–17). She wanted to eat from the forbidden knowledge tree. As she was pondering this out-of-bounds meal choice, Satan sauntered in and gave her *really* bad advice, and she chose to listen to evil instead of Good. She took the ill-given counsel and then took the forbidden fruit, consumed it, and became sin-filled in that moment. The first of history's tables were flipped, and now, Eve's food instead consumed her. She literally was what she ate. Sin had entered her innocence, and her purity and perfection were over. Now began the decaying of God's creation and the rotting away of her very life.

And, to make matters worse, Eve shared it with Adam, who also became sin-soaked that day—such a somber and heavy moment for God and for them, and of course the rest of us. Sin, at its core, is separation from God. When we deliberately choose sin, we choose the worst possible option. We cut ourselves away from the one thing we need most: close relationship with God and loving connection with others.

I was at a conference for women in Christian leadership given by Western Seminary, and the theme of the morning was "Abide." The keynote speaker said something that has never left me. She said during her powerful talk, "If we do not remain, abiding on the vine with Christ, if we start to pull away, even just a little bit, we begin to die."[5] That line is a haunting reminder for us all.

Come to think of it, our first sister, Eve, is not much different from you and me. Thousands of years separate our existence, but the temptation-ties still bind. God provides so many good things with which we can fill ourselves, good and perfect gifts meant to fulfill us and offer us wonderful things. The best one being, of course, Himself - Life itself. But, like the very first people, we often choose to pull away rather than abide, which starts us down a trap-laden road and away from true life.

We can also take horrible advice from others, ourselves, and of course, the author of lies and cunning himself, Satan. Interestingly, after Satan tricked the first earthly inhabitants, God punished the deed and made the snake, the symbol of evil, a practically silent animal by removing its legs. From that point on, it would forever need to slither along the dust to travel. Isn't that just about right? Whenever we are about to be tempted into really bad things, we don't hear a stampede of trampling hooves alerting us of incoming

41

danger. Instead, temptation silently sneaks in, with us hardly noticing. Satan is much more shadow than flashpoint. True to his character, he lurks up behind, sneaky and slithering. Oftentimes, we do not even take notice of him until it is too late.

The irony of the term "self-control" is that it is not about our act of taking control, but rather about our surrendering control over to God. It has very little to do with us actually, and immensely more to do with our willingness and desire to make God's will and design the ultimate authority of our lives. We are often at roads intersecting, struggling to choose how to proceed: following our own desires or allowing God to navigate. We were not created to win this battle alone. Surrendering control is the only way we have a fighting chance against the enemy's constant onslaught: "So letting your sinful nature control your mind leads to death. But letting the Spirit control your mind leads to life and peace" (Rom. 8:6 NLT).

Once we make the choice to yield ourselves over to faith, we are promised that one day we will reside in the restored garden with our Creator as intended (Rev. 22:1–5), but in the meantime, we must be watchful of what we allow to consume us. True contentment is being one with Christ, keeping Him as our main desire.

Psalm 1:1–4 tells us:

The truly happy person

> doesn't follow wicked advice,

> doesn't stand on the road of sinners,

> and doesn't sit with the disrespectful.

Instead of doing those things,

these persons love the LORD's Instruction,

and they recite God's Instruction day and night!

They are like a tree replanted by streams of water,

which bears fruit at just the right time

and whose leaves don't fade.

Whatever they do succeeds.

That's not true for the wicked!

They are like dust that the wind blows away. (CEB)

Sure does make you think twice about choosing a life of crime, eh?

Reading that Psalm, I sometimes struggle with the part that says the happy person "doesn't stand on the road of sinners and doesn't sit with the disrespectful." Since we are all sinners, I question if that is a little pretentious. At first glance, it seems that way. After all, don't we all have jagged logs sticking out of our eyes? I surely do. It makes me squirm a bit to read that I cannot hang with sinners, or in other words, my own kind. And I thought I was supposed to act like Christ, the "friend of sinners" in this area, be amidst them, not shun and shame them.

When we reach down into what this text is warning us against, however, new light is shed on an important piece of incredibly wise advice. The psalm tells us not to *stay* with sin. In other words, do not get settled in the La-Z-Boy recliner next to it and get comfortable. We should keep walking when we notice trouble ahead tempting us and inviting disrespect for God, not take off our coat and shoes, make ourselves at home, joining in. We must journey on using the clear instructions laid out in God's Word. Then we will succeed and stay on the right path leading to a fruitful, abundant life.

I grew up in a family of six kids, myself and five brothers. We all grew up in the same small house in a safe part of town on over an acre with room to run and tire out before the day's end. Our yard was a kid's dreamscape, complete with fruit trees, a large laurel bush cave we pretended was an exotic jungle, and even a creek. You might say it was our own garden of Eden of sorts. We went to church weekly, prayed at bedtimes and around the table, and had two kind parents who worked hard and loved us well. Mom and Dad disciplined to be sure, but only appropriately. We had a casual, fun, and chaos-filled home but that was fine in our opinion.

"You have the best family!" was a commonly heard statement from our friends. We were the house where the neighborhood kids gathered and enjoyed everything from huge hot-summer-day water balloon battles to rowdy volleyball games until dusk. And somehow, Mom always found enough food to feed everyone, which felt like a daily miracle on Dad's salary (sometimes I think she must have been able to do that bread multiplication thing like Jesus).

So yes, we had an idyllic childhood in many lovely ways. As they say, life was good. If only that is where the story stopped. "And they all lived happily ever after..."

Propel forward to today. Sadly, and to their peril, three of my sweet brothers broke relationship with God and sided with the world and its ways instead. They got tempted by evil, enjoyed its company a little too much, and kept asking it back to stay. Now, as

I write this, they are desperately trying to glue life back together, to reconstruct some semblance of the good place that was lost. One of them is now in prison, and the other two are addicted to drugs and going in and out of rehab, struggling every day not to return to the dark places that consume and destroy.

If you would have told me thirty years ago that my "perfect" family would one day be so incredibly imperfect, literally broken in two, I would have looked at you in shock and told you to see a psychologist. "That's crazy talk!" Just goes to show that life can take turns nobody would ever expect and that inviting sin into our lives has dire consequences. All are susceptible to its lure. There is no person impervious to temptation; it is a universal blot on us all.

We truly eventually become controlled by what we consume. And sometimes, if not careful, we shatter beyond what we think can be repaired. In her book *It's Not Supposed to Be This Way*, Christian author and speaker Lysa Terkeurst writes about her experience of being a happily married woman whose life was suddenly turned upside down by her husband's affair. One of the book's many notable chapters is called "Dust." It states,

> We live in a broken world where broken things happen. So it's not surprising that things get broken in our lives as well. But what about those times when things aren't just broken but shattered beyond repair? Shattered to the point of dust.[5]

This sad statement reminds me of my three brothers. Over years of not controlling desires that were harmful, their lives became dust. Due to choosing repeatedly to ignore God's way and going along with the world instead, they became shattered remnants of themselves and harmed many others in their sins' wake. Making a

45

pattern of selecting badly will eventually wrecking ball your life, sometimes beyond recognition. We must stay in God's Word to discern the right choices and be strengthened to resist the wrong. He is our unfailing tour Guide.

So, what does He expect of us? "But the fruit of the Spirit is love, joy, peace, patience, kindness, gentleness, goodness, faithfulness, and self-control. Against such things there is no law" (Gal. 5:22–23). This certainly offers us a better way. Sounds great, right? Sounds unattainable too in this real life full of very real temptations and irritations that grate.

It feels like an impossible and unrealistic ideal for me to stay all these things knowing myself and how quickly I can turn away walking briskly down the wrong road. I get discouraged that doing these perfectly will not happen; again, my type A personality rears up its head. But since perfection is not meant for us while we are still in the world, the closest we can come is by staying tethered to the Holy Spirit, He is our only hope. Still hard to do perfectly, but attainable if we deliberately choose this way instead of our own.

For example, what would our days look like if we practiced the offering of extended patience instead of quick attacks, or kind words instead of those dripping in criticism? If we chose to control our natural tendencies by fully offering them up to God with wide open hands, humbly asking for His Spirit's help? Our days, our entire lives, would be transformed, that's what.

Not all of us struggle with severe addictions, but we all still have work to do in the area of self-control. As you can probably guess, I could do with way fewer French fries in my diet, and along with that a lot more patience, gentleness, and goodness! We must prioritize choosing God's better way, or our lives could self-destruct too.

We can also do real harm to those around us, many times not even realizing it. I am speaking from personal experience and many, many times of choosing my ego's ugly and insatiable desire to be right over loving others well. I think my dear husband would agree that if there were a Nobel Prize for pushing an agenda, I would have won many by now and probably need a giant trophy case for them all somewhere in the house. I daily pray for circumcision of my pride, the golden idol I hold close and dear much too often, so I can see clearer and keep bearing good fruit.

Mark 4:19 tells us, "The cares of this world, and the deceitfulness of riches, and the lusts of other things entering in, choke the word, and it becomes unfruitful" (KJV). If we decide to listen to the world and what it tells us is good, willfully eating up its poison apples, God's truth gets choked out and the good fruit that is trying to grow in our lives becomes dead and useless.

Certainly, we will falter and fail. Trust me, I am rather good at it. But we must remember that our sin cannot replace our salvation unless we allow it to and give it power. It is our responsibility to deny its access into our hearts, minds, and choices.

Thankfully, however, even if we do shatter...God has a plan in Christ. He loves us too much to leave us as dust. He died on the cross to save us from just that. The chapter I referenced earlier in Terkeurst's book tells us that there is even hope in the dust:

We think the shattering in our lives could not possibly be for any good. But what if shattering is the only way to get us back to our basic form so that something new can be made? We can see dust as a result of an unfair breaking. Or we can see dust as a crucial ingredient.[6]

This is our deep and wide-rooted hope! Our Father will not leave us shattered and unrepaired; He will remake us from dust just as He originally formed us from it if we humble ourselves and ask Him. God will make us new. That is a promise from His Word: "Therefore if any man be in Christ, he is a new creature: old things are passed away; behold, all things are become new" (2 Cor. 5:17).

Recently, I watched a TED talk by Johann Hari about addiction, specifically heroin addiction. The speaker taught that originally scientists thought drug addiction was the result of a chemical hook in the drug. They did experiments with placing a single rat in a cage. The only things in the cage were a bottle of regular tap water and a bottle of heroin or cocaine-laced water. The rat tried both water choices and kept going back to the drug-laced water over and over until it eventually killed itself. That became the baseline of understanding drug addiction: If you try it, you will like it based on a chemical reaction in your body and then become addicted. End of story. Once you are hooked, there is no hope.

However, professor of psychology Bruce K. Alexander decided to do a revised experiment. He designed and created what he named "Rat Park." It was a dream environment for rats, their own tiny paradise, so to speak. It had lots of room to run around, tons of food, many other rat friends and toys, and tunnels to play and hide in. It also had the same bottles of water, one of normal tap water and one laced with heroin or cocaine.

What happened is very surprising. The rats all tried both waters. However, most of them did not continue going back to the drug-laced water, and none of them overdosed. Overall, they chose the regular tap water to quench their thirst, mostly ignoring the unsafe choice.

Alexander's team even put rats that had been living in the boring, bland cages with only the two water bottles for months into the Rat Park environment, and they also stopped drinking the drug-laced water in favor of the plain. They did self-withdrawal. Why? Because they were in an environment perfectly created for them to be happy and fulfilled. Bonding with others and living in a place that satisfied their other needs overrode the desire for the drugs. They no longer used the narcotics to fill themselves; they had better things now.

So, what are we to learn from this? That rats are smarter than us? No! Rats are much simpler than us. Humans have complex lives and minds touched by trauma and situations rats do not have to deal with. Besides, Satan does not care about tricking rats. He cares a lot, though, about tricking us, God's own children, into walking away from Him and therefore life itself.

The overall lesson to be learned from the "Rat Park" experiment is that when we feel disconnected and detached, we will bond to anything we can to numb ourselves from the hurt this life can dump on us in truckloads. Johann Hari also noted in the TED talk how many Vietnam veterans were heavy users of heroin during the war but 95 percent went back to living life without it once they were back in the safety of home and with the people they loved.[7]

Some people though, even when raised in a loving home with no obvious and glaring reason, still go down the dark path. This was the case with my brothers. It is hard to understand, but this world and its temptations deceive, and many will take the rotting bait no matter their backgrounds and home life.

When we choose to reject the Source of life, we reject the best part of living, and then in the deep void, something, even a thing that is really bad for us, feels better than nothing at all. We temporarily fill the emptiness, but sometimes at the price of emptying our very souls. Let's remember God created many, many good things for us to enjoy. And, when we choose to remove God's will and what He has graciously offered—the absolute best for us— we are in danger of unhealthy desires tempting us away and toward our demise.

Now, please do not think I am saying it is easy to recover from addiction if that is your story or the story of someone in your life too. Truly, I do not want to sound cavalier about how hard it is by any means, because I know it is gut-wrenching and excruciating work to walk the brutal road of recovery. I have had a heart-wrenching front-row seat watching my brothers' deep and long-standing struggles with it. But just because recovery is arduous and difficult does not mean we should not strive for it. Recovery is vital and always worth the effort, whatever our temptation is.

About two years ago, during one of my younger brother's many attempts to get clean from drugs, I went to the Life Recovery group at my church with him. After prayer and a short video, they separated the women from the men for small group discussion, and in my group, brave women began to share their stories of struggles with addiction and life choices riddled with regret. As they went around the circle and as they got closer to me, I was thinking I was only there as support for my little brother; I did not have anything I was addicted to. I sat, fidgety and nervous thinking, "What am I going to say?"

In that moment, God answered. He placed heavy on my heart

the times I had not chosen well either. I had my own versions of drugs, those things that helped me to avoid real life and numbed me. Scheduling late-night work meetings over having family time. Consuming that third glass of wine knowing that two is my limit before tiredness and haziness settle in, or worse, impatience and sarcasm with those around me. Watching way too much television when I should be offering those precious hours to the people right in my own midst. I too had issues in need of recovery and redemption. Of course I did. The battle rages on, and my urges to welcome them in and allow them to take up space continue to pursue.

God reminded me that night that we all have things that remove us from our best selves and the life He designed for us. I was humbled to be brought to repentance for the things I put in front of God and the sweet people and things in this life He created just for me. I may not have an addiction as the dictionary would define it, but I definitely have issues with choosing my own way before God's, and therefore, not choosing well.

Bottom line: An addiction or unhealthy desire is anything that makes our lives less than God's best for us. We all have something that separates and divides. We need to search our hearts and ask God to help remove our desire for it and replace it with the desire for more connection to Him and others, with the craving to choose better:

> So do not let sin have power over your body here on earth. You must not obey the body and let it do what it wants to do. Do not give any part of your body for sinful use. Instead, give yourself to God as a living person who has been raised from the dead. Give every part of your body to God to do

what is right. Sin must not have power over you. You are not living by the Law. You have life because of God's loving-favor. (Rom. 6:12–14 NLV)

Why did three of my brothers choose the paths they did? I cannot answer that for them. I do not even think they could. Remember though, God's promise is to make us new. Let's all be watchful of the choices we make so that we remain in God's plan for our lives. Friends, if we are what we eat, then let's binge on His truth!

God has instilled necessary restrictions for our safety and protection. If we give in to uncontrolled desires, we should repent and get back on His path, refusing to allow evil to fester and destroy us.

And finally, let us give thanks to God for all the beautiful choices He has given for our enjoyment and choose to surrender control. In doing so, we choose freedom from the bondage and betrayal of the world and trade it in for the One who offers us only good things.

He will not leave us dust. Now, let's not leave Him.

CHOOSING... Complex, Simple Faith

And we shall be made truly wise if we be made content;
content, too, not only with what we can understand, but
content with what we do not understand—the habit of
mind which theologians call—and rightly—faith in God.

—Charles Kinglsy

Miraculous things surround us. For example, did you know that every gorgeous snowflake has exactly six points? Snowflakes are also symmetrical and each unique from the trillions of other snowflakes falling at the same exact moment.

Flowers are symmetrical too. You can draw a line through a flower and you will see mirror-image symmetry.

Earth, the planet we happen to inhabit, is the only planet sphere in the immense universe found to have perfect life-sustaining attributes, and the odds of this occurring by happenstance are astounding. I recently read in an article, "A new study suggests that there are around 700 quintillion planets in the universe, but only one like Earth. It's a revelation that's both beautiful and terrifying at the same time."[8] Seven hundred quintillion? Just saying that number out loud feels above my pay grade. I mean, what does that number even look like?

700,000,000,000,000,000,000. Whoa.

If we really get intellectually honest with ourselves, these three facts alone are amazing enough to accept that a grand designer of the universe must exist. But of course that is not even close to scraping the surface. One single cell is so complex in design and utility that its very existence severely undermines the big bang theory. Each human cell is said to contain over ten billion proteins with various, specific purposes.

I read another interesting and compelling online article recently, entitled "Cheating with Chance," which includes a renowned scientist's thoughts on the subject:

Fred Hoyle, British mathematician and astronomer, used analogies to try to convey the immensity of the problem. For example, Hoyle said the probability of the formation of just one of the many proteins on which life depends is comparable to that of the solar system packed full of blind people randomly shuffling Rubik's cubes all arriving at the solution at the same time.[9]

I don't know about you, but even my beginning attempts at a Rubik's Cube completely frustrate me and anyone who has the capacity to solve it is, in my mind, up there at genius status. Thinking of even one blind person solving a Rubik's Cube completely boggles my understanding of what is possible, so the idea of crowds and crowds of blind people doing it is entirely impossible to accept or fathom.

Even though there are so many holes in the big bang option, multitudes of people of high intelligence choose to accept it as settled and factual truth. In other words, they believe that this complex universe in its intricate design and specific functions sprang up when a big energy event collided with a big blob of cosmic goop. And, that this collision just happened to make everything fall into place, and not only that, but also happened to make everything mind-numbingly beautiful too. For me anyway, it takes an immensely larger leap of faith to trust in that than to believe in a loving God who carefully designed and made it all, just for us. Another way to put it; anything that is designed has a designer.

Being in the interior design trade for thirty years, I know that good design is a distinct and intentional process that uses specific tools like proportion and scale, color and light, texture and balance. Buildings and interior spaces are one thing, but I can't even begin to think of something more intensely and specifically designed than our immeasurable universe—trees, flowers, insects, animals, stars, sky, and ocean teeming with color and life, not to mention human beings who can reason, love, and hurt in the cognitive and physical sense!

Evolution is founded on the notion that each living being has evolved from another to improve its chances of survival. What about the abstract, spiritual things we experience? Like dreams and imagination? They would serve no purpose in a purely evolutionary world. These are of another dimension, from the realm of the soul, where things get deeper, a bit cloudy and colored with memories and the miraculous and the unscientific. There is no formula for figuring out our conscience and our imagination. Yes, these are indeed from another place, the place where science ends and the Creator's untouchable ability and creativity began.

I heard a story one time about an evolution scientist walking with a creationist friend on the beach. Suddenly, the two stumble upon a pocket watch in the sand—an intricately designed and beautiful working piece of ingenuity, with springs and gears and perfectly kept time. The creationist picks up the watch and says to his friend, "So, if I were to believe in the big bang, I would have to be able to believe that something immensely more complicated than this pocket watch one day, after billions of years, just appeared in working order, designed to perform a distinct purpose and in a predictable and precise fashion?"

The scientist just stands speechless. He has never thought of the origin of the universe like that before.

His friend then shakes his head and says, "I can't even fathom a simple pencil jolting itself into existence like that, let alone a pocket watch."

Anything as complex as the earth, with such patterns and rhythms and exact requirements for life, cannot just come from an undefined blob. It is like putting a marshmallow in the microwave and expecting it to turn into a perfectly formed, delicious steak and potato dinner with chocolate cake for dessert. Instead, of course, in about twenty seconds, *BOOM!* It explodes all over the place. It makes a huge, sticky mess, but the marshmallow remains what it started as; corn syrup and sugar. The content, purpose, and ingredients did not change, only the appearance. It did not get more complex and organized, just messier and more chaotic.

We humans tend to think we should be able to figure everything out. Just give us enough time, high-quality microscopes, and money and we will get to the bottom of the mysterious and miraculous things. We can clone animals, separate DNA particles, and make the beginnings of babies in a Petri dish, so we think we have what it takes. However, we are still using parts and pieces given to us by creation. We cannot recreate these on our own. We cannot create new water or air or dirt or life; we can only reuse what already exists.

It seems that we have extraordinarily little resolved actually, and some are in a desperate plight to feel smarter than the One who created it all. Meanwhile, we are missing the best part of creation: The miracle, the sheer gift of it, the ability to trust that we do not need to figure it all out because God already has. Faith.

My late grandma Dorothy was a beacon of faith in our family. She, my grandpa, Aunt Gayle and Uncle Orve lived on a lovely stretched-out farm in Idaho when I was younger. It had two houses and a big barn and gardens for days. It held boundless amounts of vegetables and berries growing in the fertile, heated, well-watered soil and fruit trees to pluck from at whim. My summers as a kid were spent running around this small paradise on endless hot days, chasing the cows and chickens and feeding the pigs and feeling wonder like I have not experienced since. Warm home-baked bread slathered thick with butter was always waiting for us at dinner, and fresh raspberries, right off the vine, topped with loads of whipping cream was dessert. Those days were good and sweet in so many countless ways.

The dearest part, though, for me looking back was seeing my grandma's faith lived out. She spoke often and naturally about God's blessings and His creation and how amazing it was. While in the garden, she would take me aside, gently kneel next to me, look into my eyes, and say things like, "See, sweetheart? Look here. Isn't this strawberry just wonderful? God must have known I would be born one day, so He made things like this for me to eat because He knew I would enjoy them so much."

Her faith was a real, daily, and tangible experience, like feeling the warm dirt on your hands or the juicy berry on your tongue, not locked away on a cabinet shelf to be dusted off only on Sundays. Because of her deep faith, my mom's faith was planted, and in turn, mine too. Grandma just had a way to help belief grow, just like those gorgeous berries in her garden. She watered and tended to the seeds sown in us often in her loving, soft-hearted way, and now, thankfully, there is ripe, beautiful fruit. I will always remember her and those days with fondness and gratitude.

True faith is the absence of skepticism. It is open-mind and open-heart living. Faith takes childlike trust and being okay with not having every answer, every box checked. Jesus exhorts us, "Truly I tell you, unless you change and become like little children, you will never enter the kingdom of heaven" (Matt. 18:3). Children ask many questions, yes, but they do not have preconceived answers in their heads; they just seek truth. Adults often feel the need to be right rather than gather understanding. We sometimes throw mud on pure and true things, faith and belief being two of the most precious. We make things that are simple unnecessarily complex. God makes the complex simple. "Just believe," He says (John 3:16, author's paraphrase).

His plea is communicated over and over in His Word. We do not have to understand His love to believe in it; our unbelief does not make it any less real. Children do not ruminate on why and how something wonderful exists; they just enjoy that it does. Now, can we grown-ups do the same? We do not need to dissect it, separating skin from bone and questions from answers, just be glad in it. Accept the gift.

Little children trust instinctively and because of that are innately joyful. It is we "enlightened" grown-ups who mess them up. We rip innocence and their faith up when we pour our own fear, sarcasm, and skepticism into their spirit. We tear out the most precious parts only to replace them with doubt not meant for them and skeptical-soaked hearts.

Friends let's not. Let's choose better. To do this, we must decide to see the miracles among us. Instead of always trying so intently to come up with reasons and explanations for things, let's relax in the wonder, step back into childhood's garden. Long-worn, bruising holds are unlocked and released when we do. Faith can soften even the hardest of souls and reassure them that they too were created for purpose and love and eternity. Nobody is out of bounds or too dirty, blind, or lost to be called over to salvation's open gate and enter through.

Thinking on this, I am reminded of the story of Bartimaeus in the Gospel of Mark:

Then they came to Jericho. As Jesus and his disciples, together with a large crowd, were leaving the city, a blind man, Bartimaeus…was sitting by the roadside begging. When he heard that it was Jesus of Nazareth, he began to shout, "Jesus, Son of David, have mercy on me!"

Many rebuked him and told him to be quiet, but he shouted all the more, "Son of David, have mercy on me!"

Jesus stopped and said, "Call him."

So they called to the blind man, "Cheer up! On your feet! He's calling you." Throwing his cloak aside, he jumped to his feet and came to Jesus.

"What do you want me to do for you?" Jesus asked him.

The blind man said, "Rabbi, I want to see."

"Go," said Jesus, "your faith has healed you." Immediately he received his sight and followed Jesus along the road. (10:46–52)

Bartimaeus was a beggar with few, if any, creature comforts. His voice and faith were likely all he had. He was accustomed to using his voice to gain charity from passersby, but this time, he called out in desperation to Jesus to heal him. He had nothing to lose in this interaction but everything to gain, and you can sense his urgency. This was his chance to intersect with the God-man he had heard all about and put his faith in even before this fateful encounter. And so, Bartimaeus broke through the crowd's noise with his booming and determined voice-hammer to gain access to the One who could make him whole, and he was forever rewarded because of his belief.

Perhaps this very passage is where the term "blind faith" found its origin. That would be ironic since many atheists today use this term for belief in God. I, of course, believe faith in God is just the opposite, that the proof of God is all around us; blatant and immeasurable and impossible to miss if we just open our soul-eyes and sealed-up minds.

What about you? Are you ready for simple, pure faith? Are you just outside the gate, ready to accept Jesus' invitation to step in and see? Faith is God's access point. Don't miss the door, blinded by the haze of long-held questions you can't answer. Enter in. Ask Him to make you whole too. You have nothing to lose, everything to gain. This is a sure thing, a win-win opportunity.

Now, recline and relax. You and I do not have to have all the answers. All we need is belief that He does, and that is enough. Can't you just feel the pressure lift?

Faith can be as simple as my grandma's strawberries. In fact, it should be. It is pure beauty and sweetness, complex and simple wonder, and it is very, very good.

CHOOSING... To Forgive the Sting

Never does the human soul appear so strong as when it foregoes revenge, and dares to forgive an injury.

—Edwin Hubbell Chapin

I remember when I was about eleven years old, climbing up into our bright and gaudy green-and-yellow tree house. My dad had built it a couple of years before and secured it up into the branches of our huge weeping willow tree in the backyard. He was what you might call the highly frugal type, or, cheapskate is more like it, but we would not call him that to his face. We would just nod and grin when he would come home from the store with his latest bargain-basement find.

The odd colors of the tree house were courtesy of an "oops" sale at the local paint store, where they sold gallons that were rejected by the customer at a highly discounted rate. Well, one man's trash was always my dad's treasure, especially when he could score it for 50 percent off or more. So, our private perch eight feet above the ground looked more like a large, rectangular-shaped lemon piñata than a tree house. It had its charming parts despite its odd and unseemly appearance though, including a neat little round window that you could swing to the side to open and peek out. It was just the place to go if you wanted to get away for a while, and with eight people living in one small house, I visited the quirky, bright yellow box often.

A few years since its conception, the little house had begun to show signs of wear and tear. The paint was peeling some on the ceiling, and I raised my finger up to pull down a big flake it, and *zing!* I got stung by a nasty and irritated wasp. The pain it caused still reverberates; I remember it clearly; little stinker. When the tree house came down a decade or so later, I fondly remembered the good times and solitude it offered, but I also could not forget how that wasp had wounded me. To this day I do not think I have forgiven it.

Sometimes life lands a sucker punch, painful and surprising just like that wasp sting. Truth: people hurt people. Like my childhood tree house, this life, if nothing else, shows the wear and tear of living in a fallen world and a less-than-perfect state. The paint is peeling, so to speak, on our walls too.

Our marriage foundation cracks deeply when our spouse dashes the dream of forever with an affair that seemingly comes out of thin air. Or when a dear friend suddenly turns on us like a rabid dog and confusion and hurt move in like a pair of unwanted house guests deciding, despite our objections, to stay and make themselves comfortable for a good, long while. Or when a beloved grown-up child decides they want nothing to do with us any longer and evaporates from our life without explanation, without closure, tearing down what we've built up over a lifetime and leaving us in shambles like a bombed-out town in a warzone.

In each of these scenarios and so many others in the broken here and now, we are left holding the shards of a shattered prism of confused questions of what happened. And why? And how this can possibly be? As Christ followers, we can be made to feel that we are supposed to instantly get over things, forgive no matter what, move on now, spit-spot. Isn't our faith supposed to cover all pain and mend all wounds? But forgiving the hurts caused by others even when we still feel run over and flattened seems laughable and somewhat cruel to suggest. We are real people too, with real-people feelings, so choosing to be forgiving when all hell is breaking loose around us feels ridiculous and just too much to ask, right?

I think so. Yet, when I pause, rise up above the feelings and harmful circumstances and pain, and look down on the situation, flipping my perspective, I begin remembering God's insane love, and well, that is also ridiculous. He loves us and, yes, forgives us even when we do horrible, hurtful things. When we scream out in rage-filled fits, "I hate You! Leave me alone!"—instead of punishing us and leaving, He pardons and pursues. He chooses us and forgives us, even when we are not behaving lovably or anywhere near deservingly.

God will often and quietly, behind the scenes of our life's drama, keep holding the cue cards, directing the lights, and helping run the show even when we storm off stage in a huff over unmet dreams and expectations. He warned us this life will have trouble (John 16:33), and often that comes from those people closest to us—indeed, those we expect it from the least.

My precious, church life-group of women (whom I cannot imagine life without) had a discussion recently about how hard motherhood can be. We talked about how we felt hurt and slighted often by our kids' unkind behavior and sometimes downright mean streaks towards us. We admitted how we never thought to expect these very personal attacks, thinking naively that our kids would always think of us like they did when they were little, as their favorite people in the whole world, at least most of the time. We are shell-shocked and dismayed that their opinions of us ebb and flow, changing sometimes for the worse.

But, of course, as God's children, we do the same to Him. When we don't get our needs met the way we were hoping for we can throw some pretty hefty temper tantrums too. My Bible study group pondered why God, going into creation's sixth act knowing that we would behave the way we do, would still decide to create humans. I mean, we can be a real pain sometimes. We went rounds and rounds, playing tetherball with the topic, wrapping it up tight and unwinding it again.

In the end, we circled back to the beginning and to our own kids. And, just because we do not feel loved and appreciated or even remotely liked by them some days, we would not choose differently. If given a chance to do things over, we would still choose to be the parents of our very same kids, surprising stings and all. We thought God must feel the same.

Amazing isn't it, how forgiving we can be to our children? We get arguments, screams of hate, and slamming of doors (literal and figurative) in our face, yet we never stop loving them. This must have been a secret ingredient baked in at the beginning. Using ingredients of dust and grace, God made us able to forgive the hurts and to appreciate the immensity of when we ourselves are forgiven. This is not normal human stuff, but hallowed ground. This is the gift of our Father in heaven—that to Him we are worth forgiving, worth hanging His beloved Son on the cross for, even though we do not deserve it. God commands we forgive others so that we can be forgiven (Luke 6:37). This is something we do not get to take a pass on, no matter how much our stubborn minds and heels-dug-in hearts want to.

Confession time: I can hold grudges like they are prized possessions, and often, I bring other people down into the muck and mire with me. As the saying goes, misery loves company and sometimes a loud rager of a party feels in order. I can turn up the volume of my bitterness and invite others in for the gossiping and squawking about perceived invasions or strikes by others. Because, let's be honest, it feels pretty good to be the one in charge and the one making the charge against another, rather than the other way around.

Once, back in college, I was extremely dissatisfied with the director of the program I was enrolled in and felt she was inept and incompetent at her job. Unfortunately, I did not keep this unkind opinion to myself. Oh no, I did not. That would have been a much better choice. Instead, I made all the innocent bystanders within earshot of me hear my gripes and growling, over and over...and over. It was akin to water torture upon their souls. *Drip. Drip. Drip.* Like prisoners, they were in my dank chamber, and I was holding them hostage.

Eventually, one of my friends, fed up, confronted me and held a revealing mirror up close to my sinful heart in major need of reflection. It was lunchtime on a sunny spring day and we had just stopped at a local food truck. We each bought a huge grilled chicken burrito and settled on the steps of a park close to the school.

I thought it was business as usual; lunch with my friend who wanted to hear my remarkably interesting opinion about the director once again. How imperceptive I was. This day was to be different.

As soon as my barrage began, he stopped me in my mud-slinging tracks. "Jen! Quit!"

I looked up a bit surprised, mid-bite, sour cream dripping off my chin. "Excuse me?" I said. He continued, exasperated. "If you are not willing to do anything about changing your situation, you have no right to keep complaining about it. And I am personally tired of hearing about it." His words pulsated in my head.

I was so embarrassed.

Embarrassment can make you run and hide or make you take notice, halt and change direction. Thankfully, for me, it was a life-change light-bulb moment. I was spending way too much time in the dark, ugly room of gossip and unforgiveness. I was holding others there against their will and was finally shown the door. My friend was completely right. I had a choice to make. I was doing no good grumbling my disdain for this person to everyone else. I had made myself an unwanted guest, and either I had to change course or leave. Simple as that.

Looking back now in life's washed and wiped rearview mirror, I see things clearer. I am certain the director felt in her heart she was doing a good job, and she probably was. I let my ego reign, and I was hurtful to her and made others miserable too. I wish I would have been mature enough to rouse myself and see the error of my ways before my friend had to shake me awake. But, sometimes that is just what we need, one person willing to speak direct truth to us so the scales can fall off and we can finally see ourselves as others see us, giving us the chance to be better.

I am grateful for my friend, who had the courage to speak up and wake me up in the process. I have asked for forgiveness for my actions and learned a big life lesson: I need to stay in my lane, with Christ at the wheel. If I do not, I am sure to be tempted to turn back into the darkened room again to impart more damage to others and myself. Most of all, my closeness to God will suffer as sin pulls me back away from and not toward Him, where I desire and need to be most.

A part of the crucifixion story from Luke reveals how easily swayed we can become if focused on other's opinions rather than God's:

Wanting to release Jesus, Pilate appealed to them again. But they kept shouting, "Crucify him! Crucify him!"

For the third time he spoke to them: "Why? What crime has this man committed? I have found in him no grounds for the death penalty. Therefore I will have him punished and then release him."

But with loud shouts they insistently demanded that he be crucified, and their shouts prevailed. So Pilate decided to grant their demand. He released the man who had been thrown into prison for insurrection and murder, the one they asked for, and surrendered Jesus to their will. (23:20-25)

This is an astonishing piece of Scripture: "and their shouts prevailed." Hate prevailed. Loud opinions, unsubstantiated hate thundered and drowned out the truth and crucified innocence.

Pontius Pilate was the top ruling leader for Rome over Judea at the time. He had a reputation for cruelty and putting Rome's interests above the concerns of the Jewish community he was charged with governing. He was able to do anything he wanted in this situation, but instead of doing what he initially felt and knew was right; letting Jesus go, he chose to go along with the crowd. Instead of releasing Him, Pilate jumped in and joined the fray, seeking acceptance by the people while rejecting God Himself, even sentencing Him to death on a cross.

How often do we do something like those who accused Jesus? Gather a crowd of our own to help us jeer and spit at whatever or whomever we are mad at? In the past, I personally have done this way too much. Instead of stopping to seek God first, asking for His way (mercy and forgiveness) to take over in me and the situation, I rejected His help and redirection. I have too often let go of His hand buoying me up and chosen to swim down deeper into the dim and dark place that I think will protect me somehow.

This is so tempting in the flesh bodies we inhabit, so this is when we especially need the supernatural, spiritual side to take over and push us back to the surface where the light glints and lives and keeps us alive.

It is in these moments I need to remember and repeat David's prayer in Psalm 19:12–14:

People cannot see their own mistakes.

Forgive me for my secret sins.

Keep me from the sins of pride;

don't let them rule me.

Then I can be pure

and innocent of the greatest of sins.

I hope my words and thoughts please you.

LORD, you are my Rock, the one who saves me. (NCV)

Christ's coming to earth for the purpose of reconciliation and forgiveness is beyond comprehension because we were, and still are, unruly and unkind. One of the seven statements Jesus uttered during the six-hour agony of the cross was, "Father, forgive them; for they know not what they do" (Luke 23:34 KJV). His pleading to God the Father for forgiveness on our behalf during His own excruciating pain is shocking.

Just to utter a few words would have been extremely distressing and suffocating. I read an article about the awful reality of crucifixion, and it reads, "You'd have to pull or push your body up in order to expel air. You have to work very hard to get air out of your lungs. Breathing actually kills you because you cannot get air out of your chest." [10]

Having a savior this set on saving us and having us forgiven even though we often reject Him is the epitome of something we should be grateful for!

If you have ever truly forgiven a deep hurt brought on by the actions of another, you know how profound choosing to forgive is. If clinging to anger and confusion is a drowning of sorts, a tightening around the soul and the holding of breath until it feels everything will burst into obliteration, then forgiveness offers just the opposite; release and air, wide-open expanse. It is the breaking-through-the-surface, gasped first breath that follows the kicking and working and pushing in desperation. It can overwhelm us. This is one of life's most profound mysteries: By letting go of hate, we make the choice to hold onto love in its place and fulfill our greatest need by far.

I have a dear friend who has been through the unthinkable violation and agony of rape. And not just one instance, multiple instances by more than one person during her life. She was a young girl when it started happening at the hands of a close family member, and it continued into early adulthood by different perpetrators. Her story is difficult to hear and even harder to visualize with her. The mind will scarcely allow it. When she speaks of it, there is nothing to say in return. You are left in that space where words are useless and hollow because sometimes "There are moments that the words don't reach. There is suffering too terrible to name."[11] We cannot begin to grasp the amount of pain some people experience because of the evil choices and behavior of others, and we certainly can't comprehend the forgiveness of it.

My friend's life story is deep and rich, comprised of many layers though. These incidents did not define her, but what she did despite them happening to her does. Her decision to forgive and focus on seeking God's presence, strength and comfort through all of it is deeply inspiring. So many would turn their backs on God with a life path like hers, but she did not. Would I? I fear I may have if my life experiences were the same.

She chose, instead, to turn towards Him, seeking closeness and shelter and release from the hurt and shame brought on her by the horrifying actions of others. She made the choice to hold on tighter to God, and even though she admits she will never understand the why of it, she trusts in the One that got her through and how much she is loved and cared for by Him. She gives God full credit for lifting her back to the surface and unbinding her from the asphyxiating hurt and pain that could have held her down and submerged her for good.

This is the stuff Christ is made of. He does not stand by and allow us to remain overtaken by the waves of pain and sin crashing into and over our lives; He is a Savior through and through. The ultimate parent, He sees one of His kids aching and hurting and going towards a dark alley of hate and says, "Stop. Dear one, take my hand. Let's get you out of here."

He did this famously with the woman caught in adultery in the biblical account. The angry mob closed in on her, ready to kill with stones gripped tight, as the law of the day commanded. But there was now a new commandment: to love first, to be merciful and forgiving. Love was absent in this scene, until Jesus stepped forward and challenged the crowd with a single sentence aimed straight at the heart: "Let any one of you who is without sin be the first to throw a stone at her" (John 8:7). The hypocritical hands surrounding her opened wide, and the rocks dropped with a thud. Their hearts did the same. Christ obliterated their entire case with one sentence.

The way Jesus directs us towards right living is not with condemnation but with a looking glass raised gently up to our faces. We are told to stare at and name our shortcomings before putting others' sins on the altar as a replacement offering for our own. Scripture tells us God wants mercy over sacrifice (Matt. 9:13). We are to repent first our own sin, then forgive others. This is mercy in action. This is choosing better. We are to walk away and not keep looking back, bringing up past hurts and disappointments. Otherwise we just stay down in the pit, not up on the higher ground where we are called to be. We cannot very well be a city of light on a hill if we are stuck deep down in the mud in the valley of dark hate.

My parents were good and very consistent at bringing up past grievances about each other during fights. Many nights I would listen to them argue about things done years earlier that still burned them. Both clung to their own versions of the truth, and both seemed in total disbelief that the other could not see things their way. This spinning merry-go-round never seemed to run out of quarters, and it was an ongoing pattern in their marriage. I remember as a teenager thinking while eavesdropping on them from my bedroom, "If I ever get married, I will not do this to my husband."

Well, you know me pretty well by now. Guess what? I did this to my husband. I would let something go for a while, box it up, bring it to my mind's attic, and then pull it back into our living space when it was needed during an argument to make my own case stronger: "Ladies and gentlemen of the jury, please note and examine Exhibit A."

Flashbacks to my parents' head-spinning fights eventually started to come and stop me in my tracks, holding that mirror up to my face and my own behavior yet again. I resolved to leave those boxes unopened. Some I did. Others, I am sorry to say, still get me peeking in occasionally, tempting me to pull something out to serve my purposes. I need to haul those boxes to the dump and leave them there for good.

If love keeps no record of wrongs, then this means forgiving for real, not just burying grievances a few inches deep and then exhuming them whenever it is convenient. It is not easy to choose

73

to forgive someone who hurts us. It is possible, though, if we stay in God's loving example. There is nothing outside of God's ability to forgive, and with His help, the same goes for us.

I suppose it is high time I forgive and forget that wasp, eh? You're right. I know you're right...done.

CHOOSING... Gratefulness Up High

I would maintain that thanks are the highest form of thought; and that gratitude is happiness doubled by wonder.

—G.K. Chesterton

Today, I am overflowing with gratitude. My husband and I are on a plane bound for Mexico without the kids. Let me say that again slowly: w i t h o u t   t h e   k i d s. Pinch me and then pinch me again; I need to make sure this is real. And, I have time, specifically the coveted quiet time that has eluded me for years now, and the emotional energy to write this chapter while in mid-flight.

My typical airplane experience for an exceedingly long time included two little travelers near me requiring more snacks, more drinks, well, more everything. The luxury of typing up a chapter for a little book I am writing is just that, a complete luxury. This is the kind of thing that people without young kids have in abundance without even noticing because it is the air they breathe. That air is crisp and clean as freshly washed sheets dried in the sun, no grape juice or peanut butter stains. Ah yes, breathe it in…

I start to imagine myself as a famous New York writer on her way to meet her publisher at some lofty restaurant with a view and things like pressed bright white tablecloths and hard-to-pronounce entrées. "Foie gras, madame?" After dinner, I might catch a Broadway show. Mmm, what a life… I get lost in the daydream.

Then I remember who I actually am. The air I normally inhale is from inside my 1929 Tudor-style home with creaking and desperately scratched wood floors and an aging HVAC system. My air is shared with my two kiddos, my husband, and an extra-furry gray cat named Ruffles. I personally love that air, even the morning kind (let me clarify this: *most* of the time)—slightly sweet and tinged with the aroma of cereal and yogurt and coffee with brown sugar and the more-than-occasional cat hair. Okay, I could use much less cat hair and a new HVAC, but let's continue.

Truthfully, being on a plane with no young voices I need to stay alert for is very foreign and somewhat unnerving to my constant-mommy mind. Suddenly, I have so much "me time" that I feel odd, like my wires are crossed and sparking. My husband Mike and I have never even gone away for a weekend together without the kids, let alone six whole days to another country. Although thankful for the opportunity, I feel a little crazed and unsure, like at any moment those wires will catch fire and cause an explosion.

I can do this. I can enjoy this. Yes…I can. Breathing deeply, I settle into my seat once again, finding myself forcefully pushing mom-guilt thoughts and those bordering on ungratefulness away.

I know, I know, you are reading this thinking, "Wow, such a hard thing to be thankful for—going away on a romantic vacation with your husband." I totally agree. On its face it is incredibly lame. But, for me, being around my kids is pretty much my total world. I am very out of sorts doing something like this. This journey is about doing better, and sadly, even when things are amazing and good I can still tend to be less than joyful in my spirit. I must remind myself to continue to lean into God and be grateful, not critical or nervous or guilty, depending on the situation. Guilt can trample on gratitude like a stampede of wild horses coming out of nowhere, and I need to be careful not to allow that in all sorts of situations, even this one.

Speaking of lack of gratitude, like many of you, I am a mom and wife, which basically means being an underappreciated essential worker twenty-four hours a day. My time is splintered in one hundred directions and spent doing many things: wiping counters, tables and tears; refereeing arguments between my daughter and son (over who knows what this time); making dinner; packing school lunches; helping with math - *why* so much math?! Not to mention the work hours not contained within the walls of my house. Feeling unappreciated is a common thread in this family life stuff. We get thanked for doing a good job at work, for the wonderful effort we put into our ministry callings, and for so many other things, but a thank you card from your kids and husband for doing the laundry? You guessed it, not happening.

Sometimes, I hate to admit, my thoughts begin to go in a downward spiral. Breaking-up fantasies begin to surface when it all becomes too heavy, too hard, and too much for my limited body and energy. Too often I can feel as spent as an old dish rag that nobody seems to notice is turning a shade of gray-green reserved solely for corpses and, well, old dish rags. My thoughts then go there, to that selfish, shadowy corner in my mind: "Okay, I don't know how to say this family, but I need to break up with you for a while. It's not you; it's me. I'm so sorry. This is just not what I thought it would be." It seems this life is in constant "what needs to be done next and for whom" mode, with no mode for me. How I wish I could just push a button and switch modes at whim: "*Vrrr!* Jennifer Only mode is now activated." Um…yeah right.

In my seat on the aisle with my kids at home with Grandma, who truly should be on the living saints list right now, all I have to worry about is…just about nothing actually. That calls for major, heart-bursting gratitude, and I am trying to get there. But, at this very moment, while I slowly sip on a cold glass of ginger ale and eat from a cheese and fruit plate, I am being barraged from behind my seat by someone else's little ones singing the "Five Little Monkeys" song over and over at a high pitch that only young kids can hit. Rounds of the loud "FIVE LITTLE MONKEYS JUMPING ON THE BED!" chorus shake my brain. My calm, kid-less oasis is being ripped open and pulled apart like a pillow in a young boys' sleepover pillow fight. I start the internal grumbling and the eye-rolling thought of, "Where is your mother?"

I begin to turn around to show my annoyance, and then, just as quickly, I become annoyed at myself for feeling like this. They are just little kids, after all. Suddenly, I hear a small, motherly ringing in my head exhorting me: "Remember now, you have kids too." Ugh. Sometimes I really hate that little voice. I want to gripe and complain, but it tells me the right thing to do once again. Be still. Be kind. Be gracious. Somehow, I had it in my mind that this trip was going to be 100 percent quiet, clean, and child-free, at least loud-singing child-free. I mean, I did not leave my own rowdy children behind and head out on vacation for this, right? Oops, there I go again…

Just at the cliff's edge, before I allow the critical thoughts to settle in and take up too much space and start breeding three-headed offspring, God gently pulls me back and reminds me of who I actually am once again: a frazzled and tired mom needing to offer grace and patience to another tired mom whose life mirrors mine in thousands of ways. I too have been the one with the inconsolable, screaming toddler on the airplane who wanted nothing more than to run up and down the aisle to rid herself of the hours-long boredom that only adults should have to endure. I too have been on the receiving end of the glares and lookbacks from fellow travelers for a son loudly yelping out for more apple juice or because the battery died on the movie player halfway through his favorite video. Sigh.

When I place myself into that woman's very stretched and stressed-out shoes, I am no longer annoyed, but empathetic and grateful that this time, at least, it is not me. This time I can just listen to the song belted out in the pure-gold joy that her children possess and openly share, taking some of it for myself and choosing gratitude for it. Life is put in perspective and incredibly good. Go monkeys. When unabashed gratefulness and walking in-step with God takes precedence, there is nothing that can ruin the moment or destroy our joy.

In this, God reminds me that children are a gift and that I am pretty darn blessed to be in the club, dirty dishrag feelings and all. "Be grateful," He says to me. "There are women whose only desire in this life is to have children singing and bouncing and laughing, even bickering. You have two. Remember not long ago when you yourself longed with a broken heart for the same? Be thankful, even in the rough times."

In my natural way, I question Him. "Even when my kids are screaming and acting crazy because one of them dared breathe on the other wrong while on a car ride? Really, Lord? Be thankful for this?"

"Yes, really. In all circumstances."

"Give thanks in all circumstances" (1 Thess. 5:18) is one of the most difficult exhortations we read in Scripture. It is impossible without God's help and without our intentionally inviting Christ's Spirit to drench our days, our every moment even. We will often find ourselves in many situations that will seem ludicrous to be thankful for—illness, divorce, broken friendships, empty bank accounts, there are too many to name. However, even if we can't seem to see through the thick smog of things that are happening and feel like we are hanging from a ledge with bone-tired hands at times, we can still be thankful that we are intimately known by and cared for by our Creator, Friend-God. He lifts us up to meet His gaze, sees us, and assures us. Even in the hard, cracked parts of life, we have something very profound to be grateful for, God Himself. He is enough.

What about you? Do feelings of heaviness crush those of thankfulness for you sometimes too? My new mission is to notice and tag those things daily that deserve my gratitude and thank God for all the wonderful people and things I get to love, see, and enjoy. Identifying the blessings and being intentional about daily gratitude is an incredibly good habit to keep. Don't you agree? Personally, I know that life is indeed much sweeter when I do this.

Certainly, Mike and I will savor this week of relaxation like it was a bottle of fine champagne. We will soak in the sunshine these next few days, take naps, read books, watch movies, and talk longer with each other than normal—truly reconnect and rejuvenate. Because, at least for this week, we can. I close my eyes and thank God for the amazing opportunity, for the sheer gift of it.

I push a silent prayer up over my head for the parents behind me who do not have this sort of week ahead of them on their "vacation." It is a prayer for moments of peace and rest for them amid the sweet chaos. And I also say a prayer of personal thanks for this week of refreshment and, for the life Mike and I have waiting for us when we land back home, mayhem and all. I thank God for our crazy life with our own sing-out-loud, live-out-loud kids—the ones who make our lives so full, wonderful, noisy, beautiful, messy, and sometimes borderline insane. The scenery at home is different but just as lovely, and the air is sweet, at least to me, and I am grateful to get to breathe it in.

Being grateful is critical to joy and living contentment-soaked days. Choosing it can be tough when things seem haphazard and life splinters and cracks, but it so needed for living this life in abundance. One of my favorite quotes sits on my mantle at home, reminding me again and again, "It is not happy people who are thankful; it is thankful people who are happy."

I am indeed thankful, monkeys and all.

CHOOSING... Love in the Hard Places

When one has once fully entered the realm of love, the world – no matter how imperfect – becomes rich and beautiful; it consists solely of opportunities for love.

—Søren Kierkegaard

Love is the center cogwheel of life. It keeps everything moving, popping, and percolating. Of course, this incredibly weighty term has been severely watered down in many cases these days. For instance, speaking of percolating, loving coffee is not what we are talking about here. But to be clear, I *really* love coffee. I even go to bed at night with happy thoughts of the first cup I will drink when I wake. The rich aroma-filled mental image of filling my favorite slightly chipped mug with the perfect brew brings a smile to my fading consciousness as I drift off to sleep...yum. But this chapter is not about my inflated adoration for good coffee, even though I may be able to write a book on that too. No, loving people deeper and more like Christ is what we are exploring here.

Some people, let's face it, are just plain hard to love. There are the ornery types who criticize more than praise, who seem to enjoy making us feel small and pushing our buttons. And there are those who take and take and take and never think to give in return. It is nearly impossible to have deep, true love for these without a deliberate change and renewal of our own hearts and minds, and even then, it's not easy. And, similar to being thankful for all things, it is one of the most difficult and unnatural things we are asked to do.

Thankfully, God has given us a higher calling for love; His way, not ours:

"Love the Lord your God with all your heart and with all your soul and with all your mind and with all your strength...Love your neighbor as yourself. There is no commandment greater than these." (Mark 12:30–31)

This scripture tells us the raw meaning of life, scraped clean to the bone. We are to love God and love others. Simple in concept, yes, but not in execution. Not by a long shot.

Our natural response to the difficult-to-love is to repel, or if insulted, snap back even harder or remove ourselves from the offender and resolve to spend as little time as humanly possible with that problem...I mean person. Problem solved.

Not quite. Not even close. God is very clear about His desire that we love Him and others, and not just with a fake, mask-wearing type of love but the deep, heart-and-soul kind. If we claim we love Him, we must love those put into our lives by Him, the easy ones and challenging.

Now, I am not talking about putting up with truly abusive and sociopathic people. You also need to have love and mercy for yourself. God would never expect us to suffer at the hands of such people, but generally speaking, people are worthy of our highest calling.

We had an elderly next-door neighbor recently who was in the unmerciful hold of dementia. This caused my family many tough, time-intensive, and often confusing interactions with her. One summer day, at about three in the afternoon, I glanced out my window and saw her sitting in the hot sun on the grass outside her car, crying. I went out to see if she needed help (obviously, she did). She was hallucinating that there were people inside of her car who would not let her go into her house to use the bathroom. I must admit that inside my head I had a "here we go again" thought or two. I started trying to convince her that nobody was in her car, even reaching in the car window to show her I was touching nothing but air, but she was not believing me. She just kept talking about how badly she needed to use the bathroom and how "they" would not give her permission.

Realizing my tactics were futile, I decided to play along and pretend the people were actually there. I asked "them" if it would be okay if I took her to the bathroom, then reassured her that it was okay if she left. Satisfied, she let me help her up, and we walked slowly into her sweltering, completely overstuffed house that reeked something awful due to litter boxes in desperate need of cleaning. I slowly helped her into her bathroom and onto the toilet. I held my breath. I held her. I held on to the hope that soon I could be outside again and breathing fresh air. Mostly, though, I held my tongue.

It would have been quite easy to be harsh with her. I could have told her that I really did not have time for this again and she just needed to call someone else so I could get on with my day. Instead, I resolved to do the exact opposite, because I decided to act like the

One I aim to follow, Jesus. Following His example, going above my own selfishness and into the realm of true compassion, I was compelled to show love to her. I sat with her, talked with her, and made sure she was okay. I got her a cold glass of water and a snack. I stopped and corrected my course, alerted the Holy Spirit, before I crashed us both into the enemy's iceberg looming straight ahead, waiting to sink us. Spiritual warfare was going on inside me, and thankfully, God gripped me tighter than my own ugly pride and steered us clear.

Thinking back, I know it was God who nudged me to look out the window at the very moment I did. It was His idea to have me go out and ask, "Can I help you?" It was His idea for me to play along with the invisible people in the car, and it was His compassion coming through that kept me there long enough to make sure my neighbor's needs were actually met (love in action).

If it were up to me and my natural self, I would have looked out that window and seen her but not *seen* her. I would not have noticed her pain and especially not her need for love in a tangible sense— the real touch and time sense. Instead, I would have viewed her as an unwelcome speed bump in my day, something that I had to get over or go around but that would have hardly affected me at all. I could have easily just opted for the quick fix and dialed non-emergency 911 and allowed the police to take care of her instead. But, as I come to know Jesus more and more, I am shown a better way.

James 2:16, as paraphrased in The Message, implores me loud and clear, no minced words:

Dear friends, do you think you'll get anywhere in this if you learn all the right words but never do anything? Does merely talking about faith indicate that a person really has it? For instance, you come upon an old friend dressed in rags and half-starved and say, "Good morning, friend! Be clothed in Christ! Be filled with the Holy Spirit!" and walk off without providing so much as a coat or a cup of soup—where does that get you? Isn't it obvious that God-talk without God-acts is outrageous nonsense? (MSG)

Wow! That bites a bit, doesn't it? It says it all: practice what you preach, so-called Christian.

Jesus reprimanded the religious leaders of His time on multiple occasions for choosing to look down on others rather than look at their own sinful natures, for deciding the "sinners" were not worth their time while elevating themselves as God's chosen ones. It is all too easy to live with hardened hearts, praising God one minute and patronizing the ones He places in our care the next.

Loving well is not always convenient. It is not always easy, enjoyable, or clean. Often, it means surrendering over to what is higher, better, and outside of ourselves. This goes for loving our kids, our spouses, those super weird co-workers, in-laws, and our tough-to-love neighbors. I am grateful that God is the God of second chances, and third, and fourth, and fortieth. I am fully expecting that one day I will have another neighbor placed in my path whom I can do better with from the start. If so, I am resolved to maintain a more loving attitude. Some lessons need to be learned by repetition.

Choosing to be like Christ to others is often choosing the total opposite of how we feel at the time. That is the main point of this book, really. Jesus was a radically different human being, God incarnate. He displayed such a thoroughly unnatural (in the human sense) way to live and love people that if we truly want to show the love of God, we need to do the unnatural too. This is a job for those willing to take risks and make some sacrifices; the stay-safe and stay-clean types need not apply.

Truth be told, I like safe and clean. I much prefer comfortable and easy. But, to love on a deeper, sacrificial level is to get uncomfortable and down in the ditch (or on the grass) with someone else, then help pull them up and show that in any way needed you are there for them. This is how we live like Jesus. It is an ongoing supernatural pressing on our hearts to go into the next layer and then the next.

Martin Luther King Jr. said, "Life's most persistent and urgent question is, 'What are you doing for others?'"[12] If we are to reflect Jesus in our living, we must ask the same of ourselves. God's order of importance is not like the world's. The world tells us to put ourselves first, others second, and God third, if at all. God's order is just the opposite: God first, others second, and self-third. We all do better when we live this way.

My neighbor has since moved to a convalescent home, and I have heard she is doing well. Looking back on my time with her, I appreciate the profound beauty of the lessons she taught me. God uses hard people and their situations sometimes to teach us how to be more like Him. This is His best way to show His character through us if we choose to say yes to the opportunity. We do not need to go to some remote village in Cambodia to be on a mission field. Oftentimes, the mission field is right next door, down the street, or the lunchroom at school or work.

Easy people are easy to love, and easy to ignore or at least show indifference to. When we are faced with people who crash into our well-planned days and tidy, ordered lives is when God asks us, "Now what are you going to do?"

Again, The Message says it well:

"You're familiar with the old written law, 'Love your friend,' and its unwritten companion, 'Hate your enemy.' I'm challenging that. I'm telling you to love your enemies. Let them bring out the best in you, not the worst. When someone gives you a hard time, respond with the energies of prayer, for then you are working out of your true selves, your God-created selves. This is what God does. He gives his best—the sun to warm and the rain to nourish—to everyone, regardless: the good and bad, the nice and nasty. If all you do is love the lovable, do you expect a bonus? Anybody can do that. If you simply say hello to those who greet you, do you expect a medal? Any run-of-the-mill sinner does that.

"In a word, what I'm saying is, *Grow up*. You're kingdom subjects. Now live like it. Live out your God-created identity. Live generously and graciously toward others, the way God lives toward you." (Matt. 5:46–48 MSG)

We, indeed, are "kingdom subjects." Understanding this, we must offer true sacrifice (love in action) to those in our lives, not false mercy, like by saying a half-hearted prayer asking God to take care of them. God tells us that exercising faith in Him and performing deeds without loving others is useless (1 Cor. 13:2). We are not here to be useless, but to be on God's mission field of love.

Let us all accept our assignment to love like Christ, no matter the circumstance, no matter the person. Let us live out the life we were created for: fully loved and loving fully. It will not always be tidy or easy, but it will always be counted as worth it.

CHOOSING… Mindfulness Over Missing Out

*Beware of missing chances, otherwise it may be
altogether too late some day.*

—Franz Liszt

In this age of palm-of-hand computers, we are more distracted than ever before, in even basic tasks like driving straight or cooking dinner without burning it to a crisp (been there, done that). We just do not seem mindful of our surroundings, at least the kind that do not involve a screen.

I have witnessed more than one close call of someone crossing the street while lost in the labyrinth of their phone, oblivious to the cars that can end their life in an unannounced instant. Not until a car begins to screech to a halt are they shaken up to the realization of the danger they are in. My heart and breath stop while I watch, frozen in the space between what may happen and what I hope and pray will not. This is scary stuff. If we are not more careful, we might just walk right off the cliff and only notice once it is too late, our arms flailing and hearts racing, the outcome unchangeable.

Life is crowded with innumerable interruptions. Our cell phones, televisions, and computer screens light up and blink and seem to yell at us, "Look at me! You! Over here!" Like moths to a flame, we get enticed by the sparkling objects and stay way too long. Being intentionally present and undistracted is becoming increasingly rare and yet more significant and needed than ever. The real dirt-and-air, water-and-skin world around us is taking a back seat to our devices, and we are missing out and very much missing the mark.

On my way to pick up my daughter from school, I drive by a few city and school bus stops. Frequently, I take notice that almost everyone waiting is looking down at their phone—a lit-up, pocket-sized seductress pulling them away to look at the latest breaking news or funny video, withdrawing them from engaging with the people standing at an arm's length or less. It seems that hardly anyone strikes up impromptu conversation anymore. There is no basic small talk with a stranger that affords the opportunity to learn what their day might hold, find a common life thread, or have a spontaneous laugh with someone in the midst of the cold concrete and noise of the city. Humanity seems to be looking more and more like the gadgets in our hands—flat and impersonal.

But here's the truth: Humans are not flat. We are incredibly dimensional and interesting, and remaining personal and intimate with others is as important and needed as air for our lungs. We cannot allow ourselves to stamp out what we need the most and what we were created for, which is love and true connection.

Sadly, being truly present with the people in the life we live is no longer expected of us even by social norms. The new accepted normal behavior is to ignore. Even tables at a bustling restaurant full of lively people with rich stories to share and memories to make are too often covered with the dull overtone of indifference. Each person is focused on the object *in* their hand rather than the moment *at* hand. It is not uncommon to see two people on a date both looking at their phones and not at each other. I may be old-fashioned, but this just seems super odd to me.

How quickly things have changed (warning: I start to sound like my mother now). It was only a few years ago that eating around a table, especially at a restaurant, was considered a momentous occasion to be reveled in. Back in my day (hey, I warned you), going out to eat was like a holiday. We would get dressed up and anticipate it with glee. It was special and something we were excited about, like receiving a gift.

Having six kids and often only one income, my parents needed to save any extra money to help ends meet. My mom clipped coupons every week to make it all work somehow, and we ate more creative macaroni and hamburger casseroles than I care to remember, so eating out was a real treat. We got to go to out a restaurant meal twice a year. Once for Easter breakfast, which was always delicious, fresh strawberry waffles with whipped cream and hot chocolate served up at Coco's Family Restaurant and Bakery. And the other time was to indulge in the pork fried rice and sesame chicken at the local Chinese restaurant by the small lake in our town. We all had Shirley Temples with dinner to celebrate the occasion, and we looked forward to those outings like they were trips to Disneyland. We talked, laughed, and savored it all—not just the food, but the time together doing something special as a family. I smile looking back on it even now, missing the people we were then and, yes, the amazing sesame chicken.

Moments come around once and only once. Like snowflakes, they fall into our world and melt away without us hardly noticing.

Each one appears, then disappears, only to be very quickly followed by another. Time is precious, people. Wait, change that—time *with people* is precious. We must be mindful of how we spend our time, or we will be regretful we wasted so much of it. A cautionary wisdom nugget for us all: "Time is one of our most valuable possessions. Use it wisely. Remind yourselves often that the things that matter most should not be left to the mercy of things that matter the least."

I am reminded reading that quote by O. Leslie Stone to not foolishly fritter away too much of my precious currency of moments on things that are meaningless. Instead, I should deposit lasting, important things into my life and the people around me, investing wisely in the eternal bank and in those things that do not rot or spoil or end. Scripture tells us that love will remain forever (1 Cor. 13:8); it is what we bring with us into eternity. Love means time spent together—really together. Love means personal, eye-to-eye attention. I know I need to give more of that.

I am certain that as I live my final moments here on earth, I will not regret missing more nightly news coverage on the day's political gossip or skipping that much-touted mini-series on HBO. I would absolutely regret missing out on those warm summer evening walks with my daughter, laughing and talking about things that only moms and daughters do when alone and away from distraction and the boys of the house.

I also know for a fact that the things I'd regret most are things like not spending more time hugging those closest to me, not often enough belly-laughing until my eyes water, and not talking it out when it takes a while to get to the other side. In other words, not choosing to be mindful in the moments I am living right now. If I choose to neglect those things that make life here such a rich and beautiful mosaic, what then can I say for myself? Not much, to say the least.

I have been guilty many times of squandering moments and opportunities to connect with others. I am trying to resist, I really am, but this place gets pretty jammed up sometimes, as I tend to let too many guests in at once thinking I can give them all the attention they deserve. My phone, laptop, kids, husband, and my picky tendency to tidy up all file in, and instead of removing the ones without a beating heart, I have allowed all to remain together, elbowing for space, and my attention span gets pulled in six different directions. I can make my family feel like they are on equal ground with those lifeless objects and tasks of my affection, which is definitely not what I want to do. I cannot possibly make the people in my life feel wanted and special when I put them on the same plain as inanimate objects. They merit much better from me.

An experience a few years back showed me how important staying mindful really is, and I am earnestly trying to not take it for granted but keep it fresh and at the surface of my overcrowded thoughts. I use it as a reminder to intentionally choose mindfulness, because it is way too easy for me to falter in this.

My daughter Ashley started gymnastics when she was nine years old. She was in a class with about six other kids and they tumbled with all of their might for fifty minutes per week together. It was adorable, sweet, and pretty hilarious a lot of the time. There is hardly anything sillier or cuter than little ones in leotards jumping, leaping, and falling about. Most of the parents would sit and watch, and some would leave and come back when the session was over. One parent in particular was always there, but never present.

It was a true full-circle moment watching my daughter in her gymnastics class since my mom did the very same thing for me when I was nine. She would drive me to the local gym each week and sit there the whole time watching and smiling and waving, while I fumbled through various skills. Sometimes I would peer over to see if she saw me. She did. She saw every moment. I was grateful and knew even at that young age how lucky I was that my mom was there, not just in a physical sense, but in a connected-to-me sense. She was not going to miss it.

Truthfully, she would not have missed much if she had. It was a lot like witnessing a gawky giraffe doing handstands in a stretched-out turquoise leotard, awkward for sure and probably a bit hard to watch. I was not graceful or slender or remotely talented, but she watched me like I was an Olympic-level star and I felt like a million bucks. What a gift that was.

There was a little girl in Ashley's class, however, who I noticed was desperate to get the attention of her mom when she was performing her different skills. She was everything I was not when I was in the sport—athletic, strong, talented, and beautiful. Often, she would look back to see if her mom was watching, only to see her looking down at her laptop and that little girl got the most heartbroken expression on her face. She would do a perfect cartwheel on the beam or a powerful back handspring and then turn her head quickly to see if (just maybe) her mom was watching. She never was. She was missing it all, and both were missing out.

This happened every week, time after time. It appeared that her mom had chosen the mundane over the miraculous, traded a precious diamond for a lump of coal.

94

Witnessing this situation makes me reflect on my own life choices as a sobering reminder to choose better more often than I do. Because just as I start to stab her with my harsh thoughts of *"How could you?"* God once again speaks truth in love to my hypocritical heart: "Don't judge her. You don't know her story, and remember, you are not blameless either." I shrink down in the hard-folding chair I am perched on thinking about all the times I decided that a 5:00 p.m. work meeting should take precedence over having dinner with my family. Yes, I've certainly missed out on many moments that mattered too.

I know that for some parents a day's work schedule is not a choice and trying to fit it all in feels impossible and suffocating, so if that is you, please hear me when I say I am not speaking about you. Everyone has their own path to walk. But you see, I have a choice yet still have placed work over family time. Owning my own business gives me lots of flexibility to schedule my days in ways that could prioritize what matters, but I have not always done so. I remember how often I would plunk my kids in front of a movie while finishing up a design project I was behind on due to poor planning on my part, choosing for myself the mundane when my giggly miracles were only steps away.

I am humbled and reminded—yes, for the millionth time—we all have our struggles with this. So, Jennifer, don't throw your righteous rocks at others; they tend to boomerang right back to you. These are the more painful moments in life, when looking at my own choices stings the heart but opens the mind, encouraging grace and the door to do better.

I have a little sign hung up in my kitchen that says, "Every day is a fresh start." It helps me lift up the hope that even with all of the times I may blunder, there are as many or more chances to choose mindfulness because it is a good thing to do and this is where the best of this life happens.

We all have lots of opportunities to look at computer and phone screens throughout the day, not so many to look our kids in the eyes and let them know that we are proud of them, that we are watching and paying attention. Take time to be silly, because silly is just plain awesome and will be remembered with a smile and be invested into the love-bank we have with our kids. Or grab your spouse's hands and dance in the living room because the music calls. Living life mindfully is tuning in to those around us, and it is tuning out the rest, whenever possible. This is a worthy and valuable practice.

As a slowly recovering multi-tasker, mindful living is super challenging for me. But I have resolved myself to try my very best at making sure that when I am with one of my kids or my husband or my mom or a friend — anyone with a pulse, in fact — that is where I am fully, firing on all pistons. They have my attention. My cell phone, the television, and the like are turned off or put to the side, my eyes forward. Otherwise, I know how easily I can be drawn back in by the machines' convincing tones. "Pssst...come over here," they hiss. "I have something you need to see."

I truly believe that we have to be intentionally diligent about giving the people in our lives our full attention when we are together, especially since we seem to be together less and less these days. It is a hard thing to do when we are expected to never turn off our work selves and be readily available to the computer boss-man when the pushy read-me-NOW texts or emails come through. However, our circle of precious people need to know they mean more to us than the other matters and needs we take care of so well—the clients, the associates, the television, the car, the grind.

Even our littlest kids understand what our top priorities are. The question is, do they feel that they are one of them? We must be so careful to give them our energy and presence now because they are with us for such a small drop of time, really. Blink-blink and they have gone off to be the grown-ups they were meant to be all along, and we are left wondering how it happened right under our noses, like a roller coaster thrill-ride ending too soon. We open our eyes and say, "Wait...it's over? Already? It feels like we just started!"

In the age of mostly two-career families and time and energy being stretched and strained thin, it is hard to not take "me time" any chance we get. I get it. But I also know that I choose God's best when I choose people. My friend Sarah has many wonderful things to say, and here is another good thing she shared once with me: "In every person you meet, you can see God's face." So true and so beautiful! If we claim we believe what God says about us, then we believe that we are all made in His image and all beings to be cherished. People long to know they are important and adored by us from their first day to year 105.

On Jesus: He always took the time to stop and notice the people around Him. He is our ideal example of how to spend time with others well. When someone was hurting, He stopped. When someone needed healing, He stopped. When they needed a true friend, He was there. He looked directly at them, focused His gaze, and asked good questions and waited for the answers. In other words, He was mindful of them and their needs, and they felt valued and absolutely loved and heard by Him.

Imagine how the story of the Samaritan woman at the well in John 4 would be different if Jesus were like most of us today. Jesus would have sat there, head down, looking at a phone instead of at the woman's raw need for validation, salvation, and a life-giving relationship with Him. How many chances are we missing to offer the same?

I must believe that even if the latest iPhone had been available to Jesus free of charge, with unlimited data, He would have refused it like a temptation from Satan in the desert. Nothing distracted Him from His mission of restoration and communion with people. He was not going to fritter away the precious time He was given to walk the earth. He, after all, is the lover of souls and you cannot accomplish that looking down with a swipe of a finger on a screen.

Mindfulness means we take the time now. Watch now. Be together now. Christ's example exhorts us to resist buying into the world's cheap knockoffs and refuse to miss what matters; our real-life moments. Look up, hold them, and live them out loud—the heart-beating, tight-squeezing, belly-laughing, and salty- tear moments. Do not trade your diamonds of time for junk glass. Erma Bombeck once said, reflecting back on her life, "If I had to live over again, I would have sat on the lawn with my children and not worried about the grass stains. I would have invited friends over to dinner even if the carpet was stained or the sofa faded." Yes! A thousand times yes to this!

This life is a billion layers deep in things like good food, gorgeous sunsets, landscapes to be hiked, and long hugs. Enjoy it all, and while you do, put down and turn away from the false gods that you clutch, that I clutch. They are fool's gold, hollow and heartless with nothing real or lasting to offer to us. They are merely man-made idols of glass and metal. We should choose each day to be really mindful of spending our time and energy most often with our real people and with our very real God.

Speaking of that, time to go eat dinner with my family now. Time to turn off this machine.

CHOOSING... To Release the Prisoner

The cause of freedom is the cause of God!

—William Lisle Bowles

God's new agreement with us is this: Release. He has torn and pulled away the heavy separating cloth and weight of the law and put freedom through grace in its place. Liberation from death happened in a way that only God Himself could conceive. Death conquered death. Indeed, nobody saw that coming.

It is no accident of course that God chose that Christ would hang and die on a cross for humanity. The picture metaphor is acute and intentional. God was exposed bare, outstretched arms opened wide to offer us release from death and receive us into those same arms for eternity. The cross, once symbolizing shameful death, ultimate punishment and constraint, now symbolizes the ultimate release. It reminds us of the offering of eternal life through the eternal God who hung on its unforgiving beams, only to offer forgiveness to us all. This is an excessively big deal. The biggest of all deals, in fact. Nothing else compares.

Sometimes I forget who I am now, a redeemed daughter of God,

100

and live like this never happened, weighed down and stuck. I forget the magnitude of what it all means and stay closed-in and scrunched up, not open and freed by this gift of all gifts given to me by my good God and Savior. The Apostle Paul rebukes this tendency in Galatians 4:9: "But now that you know God—or rather are known by God—how is it that you are turning back to those weak and miserable forces? Do you wish to be enslaved by them all over again?"

Often, I find myself grumbling when even the smallest things don't go my way. My heart tends to tighten and shrivel up some if a plan goes awry. For instance, sometimes for my design work I will show clients samples of tile, carpet, furniture, and the like in a design project and they will fall in love with it all and get super excited about how their home will look. This, of course, is great. "That was easy!" I think to my proud-self as I head out the door. What is *not* so great is when I go to get the items ordered and suddenly many of them are discontinued or out of stock for months, even though just a couple of days ago they were available. I begin to step out on the shaky tightrope of irritation and defeat.

These types of things get my system easily rattled and super frustrated. "AACK! This was all figured out and now I have to re-select half of the items? Why is it *never* easy?" I lament and squawk to my frazzled self a statement exactly opposite to what I told myself just one day before after leaving the meeting.

Immediately following, I fret over having to tell the client the bad news. I worry and stew that they will think poorly of me as a designer and that I have failed them. That is to say, I stress. Of course, these are things that truly cannot be changed by me stressing out. I know that. Why is that the corner I always seem to run to then? Especially since one of my top favorite Bible verses directs me not to:

"Do not be anxious about anything, but in every situation, by prayer and petition, with thanksgiving, present your requests to God. And the peace of God, which transcends all understanding, will guard your hearts and your minds in Christ Jesus." (Phil. 4:6–7)

This verse tells us in explicit language we are not to stress or worry about anything. Rather, we are to ask God for help all the while thanking Him for taking care of it for us. Wow! And not only will He handle these circumstances ranging from the merely annoying to the very serious (remember, He did say "every situation"), He then tops off the delectable and soothing sundae with the whipped cream and cherry of peace and guarded hearts and minds—a sweet deal indeed. Talk about comfort food!

When we decide to put life's stresses and fears in first place, and not remember the cross and all that happened there and since and all that Christ offers, we choose to stay in bondage. We voluntarily remain under the pressings of the law, so to speak, and refuse the freedom opened up by the simple act of belief. It is like a pardoned death row prisoner having the bruising shackles removed but quickly saying, "Wait? I'm free to go? Nah, that's okay. I'm good. You can put those things back on."

I do this when I forget that I am free in Christ. It frustrates and surprises me that I would choose the locked chains over the unbridled mercy, but I still do it more often than I should. I easily forget about what my place in God's kingdom affords me: total release.

I know I am not alone in this; I have many fellow inmates in this hard, ruthless cell. Are you in here too? What is it about true release that scares us? Maybe it is the undeserved nature of it. We tend to feel that we need to prove our worth and that dredging through and panicking when things go wrong is just part of the sentence of living down here.

I am trying to not do this anymore, trying to be more aware of the gift. I want to accept my release papers and walk through freedom's portal without guilt or feeling like a mistake was made and they discharged the wrong inmate. When I remember and fully welcome what Christ did and still does for me the burden of it all turns to mist and I can truly enjoy my life, walking lighter with the heavy-laden backpack of fears, doubts, and shame lifted off my hunched over, aching, and tired spirit.

Speaking of release and a lighter spirit, today I am sitting here on vacation in the small beachside town of Los Cerritos, Mexico. It is a beautiful, nectar-dipped getaway along the Pacific Ocean where the land ends and the wide-open ocean begins. The air feels and smells like honey, thick and sweet.

The juxtaposition of dead and lush is strong. It's late June, and the arid desert that surrounds me is dull and practically void of color. It is like a giant paint sprayer filled with a color named *Dusty Loafers* came by and covered the whole landscape of low brush and cactus, making it all a monotonous tone of oatmeal gray. This backdrop of bland makes the powder-blue sky, deep cerulean ocean, and anything that managed to stay green and flowery in the desert stand out like a drag queen at a small town church picnic — can't miss it.

I love this place not only for its beauty and bold, contrasting colors but for who I find within myself while I am here. In this wild, color-punctuated place, I am more colorful too. Literally, because I got a spray tan the day before leaving, which made me turn a shade somewhere between tangerine and waffle cone and is admittedly a sad attempt on my part to camouflage my middle-aged dimple buns while wearing a bathing suit.

Much more important, however, is that I am also more freed in my spirit—more alive, more hope-filled, and more willing to loosely fall into the day—than when I am home living my responsibility packed, filled-up-to-the-brim life. Here, I wear floral dresses and strappy sandals and leave my hair untouched by the blow dryer allowing it to curl up haphazardly and go in any direction it decides it wants to go. Sort of a metaphor for how I am inside, released and relaxed.

The full and tight schedule is tossed out and I allow myself to lend my moments to whichever whim might take over. "Go to the beach to watch the sunset? Yes! Walk to the little stand for a couple fish tacos with that delicious avocado sauce? Heck yes! Take a long nap in the shade under the big palm tree? Oh yes *please!*" With my once rigid and structured days shattered, not only do I feel not broken, but I also feel more whole and more complete. There is something to the "less is more" theory for sure. There is, indeed, something very good in allowing ourselves the gift of release.

In the golden atmosphere of this special place, even my inhibitions about my body take a vacation. I give them all the week off, and in doing so I almost feel a tad bit frisky. No, frisky is probably overshooting a bit. I feel...much less frumpy than usual. Yes, that's it: much less frumpy. Granted, I still nip and tuck my mushy parts into swimsuits specially made with extra fabric for the nearly impossible task, but overall, I throw concerns to the wind.

104

In my cute, colorful, and slightly shorter sundresses with sandals that expose brightly painted toes, I feel younger and more alive and I find myself flirting with the world. I talk more freely with people who cross through my day taking time to enjoy their company and notice how they brighten my life. Like seeing surprise blooms in the dry desert, they are a gift. I am grateful for the discovery of each one. Basically, when I choose release, I enjoy life more. I enjoy me more, and I am positive others enjoy me more too. I focus on the good, therefore life is good. Funny how that works.

The design and colors of the desert flowers here are so intense that you can barely believe they are real. The flowers look as though they must be plastic, like those found in the yards of the elderly who do not want to bother watering the real ones anymore or maybe are just too tired of seeing things in their lives pass away. Thinking of the elderly, I realize, they understand more than most how fleeting our days are. They get just how fast life slips away and that worrying and stressing-out are a waste of time and things to be neglected, not nourished and harvested.

My grandma was one of those people who understood how precious life is. She was a master of living in the moment right up to her very last. She lit up whenever you entered the room. You could have been her favorite grandchild, the Queen of England, or the meter man; it did not matter. Each encounter added joy and wonderment to her day, and she let you know it. I want more of that. I will choose to be that way more often, seeing the goodness, expressing immediate joy in it, and releasing the rest.

Last night, I was looking out at the horizon and I began to wonder where the moon was. In a practical blink of an eye after my pondering, I noticed a bright glow of light embracing the hill directly in front of my view, and it got immense and looming in what seemed just a moment's time. In just a short burst, there was the giant full face of the moon staring right at me, deep and intense. My heart nearly skipped a beat. It seemed like God Himself was saying, "Hello there," like I was receiving a personal greeting from the Almighty. I was completely pressed down. I found myself suddenly praying joyful prayers of gratitude to God who created the heavens and the earth and this amazing moon taking my breath away, pausing my thoughts and almost my heart. I was blown away by the beauty of it and all that lay below it and hung above.

Being the sovereign Creator, God had every right to make everything just one color, or just one flavor, one shape and size, but instead, because of His love for us and who He is, He went all out, no holds barred, fully released in crazy, generous creativity. Choices! He could have just made it a bit less bland and frumpy, but that is not His nature. Instead, He made it extravagant, beautiful, and indeed, very frisky. The world is frisky, and I love being a part of it, especially when I break out of my small, confined crate fastened tight from the inside.

Inspired by God, I am going to try hard to live less sealed in. Instead, I will choose to unclasp my self-imposed shackles, no matter my location. Granted, it is *so much* easier to do while on a tropical vacation; however, it is just as important back home living in my real day in and day out life. I will open my arms and heart, take risks, taste the spices, notice the beauty, and embrace the gorgeousness of this life. I will try very hard to not waste my time here but instead drink the last drops out of my days and enjoy the fruits of His labor.

Christ died for us to live abundantly, rejecting the merciless stranglehold of the old way of the law with all its binding chains. John Bunyan, an English minister of the fifteenth century, wrote, "Run, John, run, the law commands. But gives us neither feet nor hands, Far better news the Gospel brings: It bids us fly and gives us wings."

So, want to walk out of this cell together? Turn the key for a better way of life? We show deserved honor to the Giver of our release when we do this. Let's all choose this deliverance given so graciously to us. Let us soar on the Gospel's wings, seeing and appreciating the goodness, loosening the bondage ropes, walking free.

Tacos sound pretty good about now too. Just saying.

CHOOSING... Patience in the Snowstorm

Patience and diligence, like faith, remove mountains.

—William Penn

Oh boy, here we go. My most problematic of areas: patience. We are now in the deep end. Staying patient is tough, if not impossible to do perfectly. Patience is not something we can just put on in the morning like a sweater that remains until we decide to take it off at the day's completion. It is much more like a loosely worn baseball cap that can be whipped off quickly by even the smallest gust of frustration. I am not an expert on staying patient by any means, so we will walk slowly together into the wind on this one. Hold on to your hat!

Being patient and restful is not my go-to position as you have probably gathered by now. I'm the jumpy sort, with thoughts and tweaks to thoughts going on inside my high-strung brain all day and into the night. I want to know the book's last-page secrets before hardly beginning to read the first words.

You might also call me the "get 'er done" type. For example, if a room in my house needs painting, I start the job and will not stop until it is complete, even if it takes until two in the morning. I am a bit manic, yes. I am so impatient that, feeling it takes too long for paint to dry, I will put the drapes back up while the walls are still a bit tacky. Silly, I know. I can practically feel the furrowed brows from you slow and practical types leaning towards me in disappointment. But the job is done; the room is complete. Now, on to the next item of my day. Check, check, check. I tick off my to-do list and feel the buzz of accomplishment. Some people get high on drugs; I get high on completing tasks. It is super weird to stop and read that back to myself...high on completing tasks. Oh boy.

I like things neat, organized, and clean. I love the idea of running my life like a tidy, freshly painted white ship. I have been known to even straighten up my comforter as I get off the bed, before placing my heels down on the floor. Yes...I am serious. So, you could say that the color-inside-the-lines sort of life is my thing. I am a rule-follower all the way and the overly straight and narrow sort. Frustrating circumstances easily derail me, and I can easily lose it if I am not incredibly careful.

Enter my two kids and husband. I truly had no concept of how messy kids can be and, if I am being real, how messy husbands can be (sorry honey, we both know it's true). Being an obsessively clean type did not serve me well once others began sharing my living space day in and day out. All of a sudden, I felt like I lived in an alternate universe where shoes and socks, crayons and glitter (so much glitter) invaded my peace and patience like a brigade of soldiers careening over the hill to attack a small, ordered, unsuspecting town. Landmines were planted in the form of food wrappers, clothes, toys, you name it, and my tidy existence was daily blown to smithereens.

I would enter a room, step on something out of place, and lose it—*BOOM!* I yelled at my family with rapid and surprising fervor. And even after I resolved for the hundredth time to pull myself together and act like a grown-up person should act, I would shriek out snide remarks dripping with sarcasm, like "Can't you just put your socks where they belong? It isn't hard!" or "Hey, did you know we have a garbage can? It is an amazing invention! We can put wrappers in it!"

Obviously, these moments were not my finest, but they felt good in the heat of the battle (that I was creating and fighting in solo, by the way). These cannons of criticism directed at my family gave me a couple seconds of internal satisfaction, but sadly, all my kids got was the ranting of a mad-mom and my husband more than a few headaches and probably some second thoughts as to his choice for wives. Since patience was missing in action, so was peace. And because of me, my home was not enjoyable and light and happy, and that irked me when I would finally stop the barrage long enough and look in the mirror.

It sure was different than I had imagined as a little girl picturing her "perfect" home and "perfect" family to go with it. My expectations were unmet. They were totally unrealistic, of course, like I expected to live inside of a snow globe or something, impenetrable to real life and the messes that go with it.

Every time you shake a snow globe, the snowy chaos brings something enjoyable and lovely to watch for a few moments and then settles perfectly back in place...all by itself. Real life, I discovered, was nothing like this. My real life felt more like an out-of-control snowplow spraying me without warning with its muddy, wet deluge at high speeds. I needed help. God of course, knew it before I did, and He intervened. I remember it like it happened just a page turn ago...

Ethan was almost two years old and Ashley was close to five. Life was disheveled, busy, and loud. Keeping up with the kids and their clutter-filled wake was a full-time job, and I also attempted to run my interior design business from home—emails, phone calls, drawing sets, deadlines. I was frazzled. Threadbare, really.

Thankfully, I had been going to the women's Bible study at my church for a few months and my mind and soul were getting primed to listen for God's voice. I learned His Word and His ways and why I should follow closely. He was breaking through my hard shell with the help of other women and their stories, but mostly through His own.

I believe that God sends us messages just when we need to hear them most. And sometimes I wonder if He holds His breath a bit waiting to see if we will decide to receive them, especially with me. I received one such message in the patience department. It was a very important pivot point in my life and my family's life, and I am so thankful I stopped just long enough to hear God's heart for what He wanted me to do: Choose better. Make a change.

Soon after joining the Bible study, I was listening to a radio program and the host was talking about how she and her husband and their five-year-old boy went to the state fair one hot summer day. It was a yearly tradition for them, and their child was super excited about it. She was generally a stickler for eating healthy but allowed him to get a soda pop as a special exception that day. They each got a cold drink and started making their way through the rides and carnival games.

Shortly after getting their sodas, her little boy dropped his all over the dirt ground, making a big, sticky mess. Immediately, her husband pounced, annoyed and loud, with "How could you do that? You need to be more careful!" and similar demeaning statements. Their little boy just cried and felt shame, embarrassment, and disappointment, and the joy for the much-anticipated day was wiped away.

The boy's mother, in her wisdom, chose patience and filed the incident away until they got home and spoke to her husband privately about it. She said, "Honey, if I would have dropped my drink, you would have said 'Let's just go get you another one,' but with our son, you shamed him and powered over him. It was an accident; he didn't drop it on purpose."

I heard her say those words and something in my heart snapped, waking me up like a 3:00 a.m. thought: Of course! He was just being a kid! Sometimes things just happen, especially with kids who are not like me; cautious and wound up tight. Children, thankfully, are light and silly and loose in the way they interact with the world. These characteristics are what it means to be young and what makes them so delightful to be around. I tucked this wisdom treasure away in my heart and mind, but it was never far from my thoughts.

I contemplated the radio host's words and prayed over my behavior in similar situations over the next few days. I asked for forgiveness for the times I was not gracious with my own kids. I also asked God to help me be careful not to trample over my family because of my inflated expectations that things stay "just so", in line with my idea of perfection. That was my own clunky burden; it was unfair of me to make them try and carry it too. God revealed to me that week that when I am impatient and high-strung, I am running my loved ones over in my bus full of impossible expectations. I was the problem, not them. God was renewing my mind.

Later that week, the house was clean once again. I mean, really clean. The kitchen was especially gleaming on that spring day in 2010—a day that changed my life and injected peace into our home in the most outside-the-lines kind of way. I had some extra time while Ashley was at preschool and Ethan was taking his long mid-morning nap. I scrubbed and wiped and made counters and floors shiny and bright once again. I vacuumed and mopped. I relished being tucked back neatly inside the lines of orderly life, even for just a little while.

When Ethan awoke from his nap, I played with him awhile and then gave him some pots and pans and a rubber spatula to bang on them with while I went across the hall to look at a couple of work emails. *Bam, bam, bim!* He was having fun and I was immersed in the emails, until suddenly I realized... "It is *way* too quiet." Ethan had stopped playing his makeshift drums. "Oh no," I thought. Quickly, I went back to the kitchen, and nothing—I mean *nothing*—could have prepared me for what I found when I walked in there.

My small but surprisingly strong boy had somehow pulled the large bag of baking flour from the bottom shelf of the pantry and...was...making it snow. And when I say snow, think blizzard. A baking flour whiteout inside my ever-so-recently CLEAN, SPARKLY, SHINY KITCHEN!

Now, I know myself, so I am certain what came out of my mouth that day was not me talking. I am positive that it was God, using my voice box and His Love-Spirit. Because all I said, with a big and very real smile on my face, to my little boy was, "Well, aren't you just having the best time!"

He really was! Ethan looked up at me matching me smile for smile and giggling and wiggling at the wonder of the fluffy white powder-snow floating all around him like he had discovered the key to happiness. He was beaming. I was in shock. Thankfully, God was in control and kept me in control too.

I picked Ethan up, gave him a laugh and a squeeze, and let out a big sigh putting the flour back in the pantry…on the top shelf this time (I mean, it was a cute moment and all, but I am not a glutton for continued punishment people). I looked around and got to work cleaning the flour off every surface and nook, out of the cracks and powdered crannies. I also thanked God—big time. I did not know what had just happened, but I did know something changed. He had shown me a better way through.

God had reminded me not to snap, yell, and choose frustration and anger, but rather to choose patience and love and therefore invite peace and give it space to settle in. He showed me through my little boy that day that I can indeed choose during life's messy moments to see the beauty and joy in them, not always label them as an aggravating situation and a mess to clean up and a reason to snap.

That fairground story that had been churning and turning over and over in my heart during the week prior actually became my beacon in the snowstorm, showing me the way out from my unkind tendencies and into the clarity of God's character. I chose better that day with God's grace and gentleness-filled help. I chose not to crush my little boy's spirit and risk changing him in unpredictable ways by chiding who he was, just a darling, curious kid. In turn, he did not feel fear of me because of my impatience and disappointment at my expectations' being smashed. We had a sweet memory moment that I will never forget and, more importantly, never regret. I have reflected on it many times over the years and it has kept me steady on more occasions than I can count.

We found out a couple of years after that momentous day that Ethan has high-functioning Autism. His little body could throw tantrums that would shake the house. He hit, threw, kicked and screamed, sometimes for hours. If I had chosen to reject God's earlier lessons for me and stay as I was, I am certain I would have lost my temper over and over and hurt him in ways that would have done real, lasting damage. I would not have physically hurt him—no way—but I would have given irreparable blows to his heart and mind for sure.

I cannot tell you how grateful I am for God's intervention that day and for His proving to me that when we choose patience, we all gain. Peace triumphs. Love wins. As a young child, Ethan could not communicate frustration in simple, clean sentences, so he raged. The old me would have returned the same. In those moments, though, thanks to God, instead of raging back in frustration and exasperation, imposing my expectations on my child who could not express himself in the typical ways, I just held him, rocking slowly and saying, "I love you. I love you. I know you are upset. I love you." The Holy Spirit had given me supernatural patience practice, and with His constant guidance, my sweet son and I got through many storms.

The irony was not lost on me when I finally realized what God had done. In His great wisdom and clever way, He had paired me; the most inside-the-lines person, with the most outside-the-lines type of kid and changed me for the better. Amazing grace.

Your life looks different from mine, but not so different I bet, when we peel away the outer layers. We all have people in our lives and situations that crash in and make patience difficult—those people who push our buttons hard and way too often and the daily situations that lend themselves to impatience. My challenge to us all is to remember to choose better when these moments disrupt our peace, before we get to critical mass. Let's speak lighter and show love more. We should often stop to sit at the feet of Jesus, listen to lasting wisdom, and then actually do what He tells us.

God removed my lust for impossible perfection, exchanging it with a longing for peace. And if I want peace, staying patient is key. What a difference it has made.

Maintaining patience is super hard, yes, and it is a daily fight between our natural and supernatural selves. But anything is possible when we rely not on our human nature but on God's: "Be completely humble and gentle; be patient, bearing with one another in love" (Eph. 4:2).

Hold that wise counsel high, like a lantern guiding your path, especially during life's storms. We can do this. We can choose to stay resting in His peace and choose patience, outside the lines of us, inside the lines of Him.

CHOOSING... Hard Surrender

I thought how unpleasant it is to be locked out; and I thought how it is worse, perhaps, to be locked in.

— Virginia Woolf

Kids changed me.

Life before kids was pretty carefree. I had visions of being and doing all sorts of crazy things without a worry in the world—well, not big, consequential ones anyway. Maybe I would move to some big city and be a high-rise girl who rode the subway, or to a little beach town and learn to surf the unpredictable, curling waves. I was free and unencumbered. Life was my oyster shooter, and I was going to enjoy it to the very last sweet and salty drop. I did not have many material possessions, but that did not matter. It only meant I had less to worry about.

Mike and I met when I was nineteen and he was twenty-two. We eventually married and lived this carefree life as a couple well. We went to late-night movies and out to dinner with friends and to the local river once summer turned up its heat, taking our old seventies era speed boat out on full sun and full-day cruises. Water skiing and sand volleyball filled our days. We stayed out past dark, often stopping at the floating restaurant nearby for the tail end of their amazing happy hour. "We'll have the coconut shrimp and two Caesar salads, please. Oh, and a cheeseburger!" We did not worry about calories or time; we just let both happen and savored it all. Oh, what wonderful things youth holds, or rather, lets go of.

After about four years of marriage, we decided it was time for kids, but much to my surprise, it did not happen for a very, very long time. Month after month I was disappointed and heartbroken. I just could not understand why we could not conceive. Afterall, my bloodline was *very* fertile. It seemed like all the women in my family had to do was think thoughts like, "Hmmm, I think having a baby sounds pretty good," and then poof! Pregnant! Well, not me.

I tried everything—the right foods, temperature checks, correct timing, staying away from hot tubs and caffeine — but nothing worked. It made me a little nutty actually. I was like a mad scientist of sorts, mixing various potions and suggested formulas, drinking this and not that to make my vision come to life.

About three years into our failed attempts, we did fertility testing, and it showed that everything was normal. This just maddened me even more, because if things were "normal" we would have been pregnant a long time ago. I was lost in my own miserable maze of thoughts, full of dead ends.

Often when I saw a young mother with her baby or a pregnant woman bursting with life, I struggled with the classic, time-honored question, "Why not me?" and awful, mean-girl thoughts like, "*Her?* She doesn't even look old enough to care for a child. Is she even ready?" I asked the Lord in my desperation, "Don't You want me to have kids? How can the one thing my heart truly desires now be out of reach?" I was tired of trying. I was on my knees. I was also at the very end of what I knew to do, and I had no choice but to surrender it over.

Finally, I told God, "Okay, not my will but Yours. Not my timing but Yours. I am giving this to You. I am done." I opened my hands and relaxed my heart, setting free my tightly held desires and futile pursuits into His awaiting fingers. As hard as it was to release that over, I knew that holding on so tight was not healthy and certainly a far cry from God's desire for me. My heart was broken, but I could not wrap my whole life around something that may not ever transpire. I had to move on and truly trust that if it were meant to happen it would. I do remember feeling lighter and less burdened once I trusted the result to Him. Not joyous by any means, but lighter.

Now, I know this is not everyone's outcome, and I truly wish with all my heart that it were, but it was mine: the next time I took a pregnancy test about two months later, it showed positive. We were pregnant, clear affirmation on the test spelled out for us. I took two more tests just to be sure. We were in such a surprised state that day. I realized that it was not until I waived the white flag, giving up on my own self-driven striving, that God said, "*Now* you are ready."

My slow-learned lesson here: I had forgotten to give God the chair of honor in my life. In fact, I did not give Him a place at the table at all. Instead, I filled the chairs with my own pride idols, coveting something that was blinding me to what was most important, which was not *having* a child, but *being* His child. God reminded me that He is able, and His timing is indeed perfect. He was teaching me surrender. Finally, I gave Him the chair at the head of the table and the world was right again, no thanks to me.

I relished being pregnant. It was like I was walking on clouds (okay, at the end there more like lumbering and waddling), and I got to eat the food quantities of a rhinoceros with good reason for once. I did not worry about most things during that time and just took life in stride overall, sipping from the full glass of blessings and loving life.

Things took an extreme, whiplashing pivot however, once our daughter was born. My once open and easy-breezy life turned careful and tight, almost overnight. I suddenly became terribly fearful. Was she eating enough? Was she secured in her car seat correctly? Were we cut out for this? We had Ethan a couple of years later and having two kids made us doubly blessed and me doubly worried.

Once a child is written into your life's screenplay, you no longer are the sole creative director of your days; you have a little co-writer involved in the project now. Having a child makes every decision you make feel weightier and more important and creates in you a need to think of this other human being all the time with no intermission.

Someone else is in control of your thoughts, words and deeds now. Somewhat like a puppeteer leering over you, they hold the strings in one hand and a mini taser gun in the other. Always at the ready to tangle the strings and press the button at any moment and change your best-laid plans. It is shocking indeed.

It is as if you have just agreed to be a part of a study for which they will zap you with volts of electricity every time you have a decision to make and on top of that, come to think of it, every time you finally get to sleep or want to take a shower or go to the bathroom. Zap! Zap! Your old life is gone, a new life is here—your child's, yes, but also your own that has been turned inside out and topsy-turvy. It is a bit unnerving.

I was comfortable in trusting God for all sorts of things, until I had my kids. I trusted that somehow everything would work out, and sure enough it did for the most part. Once becoming a mom was a part of my story though, I found myself unsettled all the time, like walking up a slippery, steep hill. I just could not seem to get my footing. I was laden with the what-ifs and many heavy questions beginning with the word *will*. Will they break a bone? Will they get kidnapped? Will they get cancer? Will they get bullied at school? My worry list was an overtime task master that kept me busy being burdened and stressed-out. Trusting God with my kids was not easy, or even remotely possible for me for a very long time, and I still struggle in this area, if you want to know the hard truth.

Writer Elizabeth Stone once wrote, "Making the decision to have a child – it is momentous. It is to decide forever to have your heart go walking around outside of your own body." Accurate words. Not until they crashed into my world like an asteroid I hardly saw coming and filled the deep crevasse in my life I hardly knew existed prior, did I understand how accurate they are. Bump-bump, bump-bump—now my heart was beating in the palm of little hand; pudgy fingers wrapped around it squeezed tight.

My previous life with its carefree-living days was a thing of the past. Now, molehills became staggering mountains in my mother-bear mind, or I should say, my mother-overbearing mind. Instead of allowing myself freedom to enjoy the ride, I became like a severely knotted string at the end of a kite with no way, it seemed, to get untangled.

My desire was to let my kids fly unfettered, but my anxiety held us all down. I feared what may happen to them in this big world when I was not watching. With my mommy-lenses in hyper focus, I only thought the worst possible outcome would occur if they were even for a moment out of my ever-vigilant sight while we were anywhere but inside the house, safe and sound with perimeters secured.

I thought I was protecting. But really, what I was doing was pulling the chair out from under God yet again. I was removing Him from the table and giving King Worry a place of undeserved honor instead. I let fear overrun my life and my trust.

I had to tread carefully so my kids' hearts would not be laden with worry too, but I am sure they sensed it some. They were made to soar, after all, not flounder with clipped wings of my making. For them to enjoy their lives, I needed to relax in mine. I needed to choose full surrender. That meant yielding them to their journey and to God and trusting in His ultimate plan for them, which was only His to give, not mine to take away.

I was given the ultimate test of surrender a week before Ethan's second birthday. It was a nice summer morning, and the front door was open with the screen door locked so the cool, fresh air could fill the house before the heat of the day arrived. I walked into the kitchen with Ethan toddling close behind me. He picked up the cordless home phone and my cell phone off the counter and took them out to the living room to do what we had role-played a hundred times, "call Grandma."

I went to check on him about five minutes afterwards and noticed the two phones sitting on the doormat and the screen door wide open with Ethan nowhere in sight. It was my worst fear come true. He was out of the house, out on his own, without me. Even as

I type the words a decade later, my heartbeat quickens at the terrifying memory of it.

I rushed out the door and ran the usual lap around the neighborhood that we walked almost daily thinking I was bound to find him on the known and well-beaten path, but he was nowhere to be found. A stampede of dread covered me. I felt suffocated. I prayed a panicked prayer: "Jesus, I need You! Jesus, please help me! Jesus, please keep him safe!"

Suddenly, I felt like a small child myself—a lost child in New York City. Nothing made sense, buildings and objects loomed over me, taunting me with uncertainty and dread, and I was scared out of my mind. You never know how big your neighborhood can feel until your little kid is out in it by himself.

I called Mike frantically and told him what had happened, and all he said was "On my way!" Thankfully, his shop is only about ten minutes from the house. He got home in record time, cutting the minutes in half.

I had always prided myself on being the one who could handle everything. I was responsible, organized, and on top of it. Nobody had to worry if I were in charge; all would be well and under control. My husband, on the other hand, was the overly easygoing parent who left doors unlocked and let the kids eat ice cream for breakfast. In my grossly inflated ego, I had made him feel small and subpar in his lack of parental judgment when I "caught" him doing these things. I felt he clearly needed to be shown and told by me once again how to keep our kids safe and sound and in good health, because, of course, I was the parent who did everything right. That was what I thought at least.

123

This day proved me very wrong, however. I was horrified and shaken terribly that on my careful watch this could still happen. I had failed miserably at protecting Ethan; failed at my most important post. It was a scary, gigantic slice of humble pie à la mode served up just for me. Personally, I like banana cream much, much better.

In that crazy space of time, with Ethan missing, I froze and was completely useless. It was like someone put my brain into a bucket and filled it with cement. I could not even think. Mike however, was spot-on perfect in the way he handled it. While I was stuck in the quicksand of fear, motionless and balled up, Mike was a champion warrior. Fierce and unabashed, his feet moved swiftly, ready for battle. He knocked on neighbors' doors, ran from house to house asking loudly and boldly if anyone had seen a toddler, and yelled out, "Hey! Have you seen a little boy?" to anyone in earshot.

About fifteen minutes after our July summer-day nightmare began, Mike called me to let me know he had found Ethan, and after hearing those words, I just totally lost it. Dropping down to my knees, I could not stop heaving and ugly crying for about ten minutes. I was a puddle of very relieved and grateful mush.

That day changed the way I spoke to Mike about his parenting style. I was not so perfect after all. I can only imagine if it had been the other way around and he had been home with Ethan that day and this had happened. He would have never heard the end of it. Once again, God was teaching me grace. Give grace, get grace. It makes the world go around, and we all need it desperately. Mike has never once thrown that incident back at me. I married one heck of a wonderful man.

Our miracle-helper came in the form of a nice lady on her

morning break from a shift at the hospital down the street. She was on her porch and noticed a little blond child way too young to be alone. Knowing something was not right, she brought him into her house and called 911, letting them know her precious and unique discovery. Upon hearing Mike yell out his urgent questions, she popped out and answered excitedly, "Yes! He's right here!" pointing to her front door.

Relieved, Mike ran up her steps, and Ethan was standing in her doorway calmly licking a lollipop that she had given him. All he did was point at Mike and say matter of fact, "Daddy!" as if nothing had even happened! Of course, to him, nothing had happened. The only difference that day was I was not with him on his walk around the neighborhood, and he got the added sweet bonus of meeting a nice lady with an extra lollipop. In his opinion, I am sure, it was a wonderful way to begin his day.

I thank God often for my husband's bold side that sent out the alarm and our neighborly guardian angel who found our son and kept him safe that day. Ethan got a lollipop, but I got something too. I got back a part of myself that had been lost for far too long: the ability to offer grace and relax and surrender all to the God who sees me. He had heard my cries, He sent an answer, and He showed me His faithfulness.

That day reminds me of the story of Hagar from the book of Genesis. She and her son were lost and scared as well. But God was there in their midst, giving comfort and direction. After God spoke to her, Hagar called Him, "the God who sees me," because, she said, "I have now seen the One who sees me" (Gen. 16:13).

True, I was not side by side with Ethan that day watching his every move and protecting him, but God was. God had nudged someone kind to look up and see him too, out on his own, a young one lost. He was guiding my dear, unknowingly runaway son back home to us. I was shown that just because I do not feel in control does not mean He is not. He has not left me stranded and my life and my kids' lives to the random whims of chance. He is in it in all things.

God and I had a heart-to-heart conversation soon after this unforgettable day about my deep need to surrender to Him. It was just after I read the Bible verse, "If you want to be perfect, go, sell your possessions and give to the poor, and you will have treasure in heaven. Then come, follow me" (Matt. 19:21).

"Is this really what you want from me, Lord?" I asked. "To sell all of my possessions? To offer all I have on the altar for sacrifice?"

I heard in my spirit, "Have I asked you to do this?"

"No," I replied.

"But what if I did? Would you still trust Me? Would you stay with Me if I chose to take everything away?"

This stopped me in my tracks. I had to make a decision. Like Job of the Old Testament, I was given a choice: choose God and give Him control and worship no matter the hard turns and painful falls and horrible moments, or allow the enemy's lies to gain a foothold in me. I made an eternal pact that day with God and myself. I resolved to surrender all I had and to trust in life's mystery and in the good God who leads me through.

The most significant thing I surrendered was my fear-grip on my kids. I had previously justified my worry and tight hold on their lives using love: "I just love them too much, so it's okay." But it was not okay. It was taking something wonderful from me, and worse, from them. We were weighed down, missing out on lighter living and the freedom found by living in faith.

What about you? Is there something God is asking you to surrender to Him and His control? What is tugging on your heart right now as you read this, making you squirm a bit? Is there an area of your life that you hold way too tight with clenched hands and heart also? Maybe it is money, a job, a relationship or position, maybe the fear of failing? Can you take the unsure steps forward in shaky faith with open palms and exposed heart to offer whatever it is to the One who is able to do marvelous and miraculous things with it?

Certainly, this is far from simple. I have learned that firsthand. It is one of those daily struggle items for me. But, each time I do, it helps push the unbelief and fear away more and gets me closer to actual rest and true peace, and that is something worth giving attention to.

Jesus asks us to come to Him when weary and burdened to receive rest (Matthew 28:11). This is not just a half-hearted offer of a holy pit stop we can take before continuing life's arduous journey. He is telling us to stay, empty out our overloaded bags and lighten up each and *every* day. We cannot truly get rest until we remove (surrender) the things dragging us down.

What an amazing offer! He basically says: "Give Me your fears, your terrors, your doubts, and the things that cause you all of those sleepless nights, and in exchange for this useless trash, I will give you rest." Jesus is, indeed, immeasurably generous. Let's not forget it is we who forget His generosity, not Him. He is always ready and willing to give us this opportunity for peace and light living.

Now, once again, I am standing at the precipice of needing to choose to surrender with our daughter, Ashley. She is nearing the outskirts of her days of living full-time in our home, only a few short years from leaving to become her grown-up self. It hurts my heart when I think too long on it, and it scares me some too. Again, honesty here.

Even though I have chosen to release my kids into God's care, there are still those moments of fear and mistrust that creep in, churning and twisting me. Like I said, this is a tough and daily choice still. Ashley's future is shrouded in uncertainty, so my controlling, overbearing side rises, and fear-ridden inquiry bubbles up. "Can I really trust her out in the world, Lord? Will she know what to do? Did I guide her well enough? God, do You have her back like I would?"

Of course, this is only my ego talking once again. I need to hold on to the knowledge and truth of who the great I AM really is; all-loving, all-knowing, and all-encompassing. He is infinitely more qualified than me for this job. I need to go on a serious, extended sabbatical and allow Him to take the position over. Funny thing is, He already has. I must realize it and relax and stop looking back over my shoulder. After all, God is a parent too. I need to remember that He loves my kids even more than I do (as hard as that is to fathom). I must trust in His much more capable hands and seeing eyes to care for them.

Just as our hearts are now in our own children, walking around separate from us but never completely severed, God's heart beats in each of us too and ours in His. He is the Good Shepherd, and this is what He asks us to do as parents—help co-shepherd our kids as well as we can for a time and then release them fully to back Him, bidding them to fly. They are only ours to hold hands with for a brief flutter of time, and then they eventually go out into the big world without us, just as Ethan did that day and my daughter will all too soon as well.

Remembering that they are never truly alone gives me pause and rest and helps me to choose to surrender with a calmer heart. And, as you probably realize by now, this is just what I need.

Today I fly the white flag of surrender and offer up the chair at the head of the table of my life once again to the only one who should sit there: my good God who sees me and all else, in all things.

Now, let's just hope I remember to do this tomorrow too.

CHOOSING... Goodness & Kindness: Mercy's Offspring

I expect to pass through this world but once. Any good thing, therefore, that I can do or any kindness I can show to any creature, let me do it now. Let me not defer or neglect it, for I shall not pass this way again.

—Stephen Grellet

Kindness and goodness—these two attributes just belong together. Like peanut butter and jelly, apple pie and ice cream, you can hardly separate them without something feeling amiss. They are like two sides of the same spiritual coin. It is impossible to imagine being good to someone without also being kind, and vice versa. You do not offer to buy someone a meal out of the goodness of your heart and then yell bruising words in their face as you hand it to them. That would upend and spoil the nice gesture completely. You may as well just throw it in the trash. When we are good, we are kind. When we are kind, we are good - they are an entwined and interlocked rope of wonderful.

It seems the Greeks could not separate goodness and kindness either. The singular name for this pair of desirable traits in the Greek language is *agathosune*, defined as "an uprightness of heart and life, goodness, kindness."[13] I don't know about you, but often this feels like a towering goal for me to achieve especially when life scrambles and scrapes and I forget how to act and think. It almost feels like something only achievable for someone living in a monastery, separated from the daily strains and toils. Removed, up on some high mountain with nothing but reflection and prayer to fill the hours and the heart.

However, if you and I in the real-world hope to live as Christ did, then we must be upright, kind and good to others. And in order to do that, we need to lift our eyes and our hearts above the horizon line of our own self-importance and daily blender of emotions and busyness that overtakes. It is like living the lifestyle of monks but we must do it right down here in the gritty moments, staying in goodness-filled grace amidst the mess.

Upright living beseeches us to look upward to God, seeking His wisdom in our daily comings and goings all the while not looking down on others. It asks that we see people—really see them, not just our potentially skewed versions of them. We cannot very well be looking down on others, critical, picky and aloof if we want to actually live out agathosune.

Mother Teresa was a wonderful earthly example of what this looks like as a daily practice, a form of true worship. She was kind in the most important of ways; she met people's basic needs of food, water, and healing of outer wounds, but even more, their need to be seen and heard without preconceived judgment. She understood deeply that treating others well in God's eyes meant seeing them as though looking into a mirror – incredible, loved and made in His image.

When we look at others in light of ourselves and who created us all, we are equal. Hearts begin to beat in unison, and true goodness and kindness can grow. Mother Teresa, this saint of the slum streets in India, made people feel truly loved by being with them—not over them, ahead of them, or behind, but in a steady, easy step alongside them. Each person she helped felt like a dear friend, a sister or brother, not a burden or a bother. True love was felt in the form of her merciful, goodness-laced touch.

She once said, "Spread love everywhere you go. Let no one ever come to you without leaving happier." Simple words by nature, but this advice requires most of us to make radical changes to our ways and our thinking. Making sure all with whom we come into contact during a day leave with a smile, feeling loved, is not exactly easy.

When I read about Mother Teresa's life lived out on a higher spiritual elevation, I am reminded of what has been asked of me by my good God:

"The LORD has told you, human, what is good;

he has told you what He wants from you:

to do what is right to other people,

love being kind to others,

and live humbly, obeying your God." (Micah 6:8 NCV)

Mother Teresa, it seems, had that "love being kind to others" thing down. I will try to emulate her, and surely fail, and remember to keep trying, because if I want to also emulate God in His character, this is not a loose suggestion but a foundational precept.

If we really love doing something, we do it joyfully. We look forward to it, sometimes counting the moments until we get to do what we love.

For instance, I love reading. It is a top-of-the-chart, preferred activity for me. I relish the days that hold enough open space so I can indulge in it. On cooler days, I light the candles on the tray sitting atop my worn leather ottoman, turn the light on over the sofa, cover up with a soft, billowy blanket and sink into the couch for a while, tuning out the world, connecting my soul to others through words and time, story and scripture. On warm, balmy days it is done on the patio area under our deck where I can look out to the garden. I release and relax, breathing in the fresh air and the words that soothe. It is my therapy form.

Again, since I love reading, I do it without having to think twice. To "love being kind to others" is to reach into the supernatural place where Christ resides in us and remain open and willing to the Spirit's calling. He is nudging us in this verse in Micah to go beyond our normal state. This is not a natural human response but is spurned in us through His power that we have been given full access to in the Holy Spirit.

I remember an awful injustice that happened back in 1998. It was done to a young gay man named Matthew Shepard, a twenty-one-year old student from the University of Wyoming. He was tied to a fence, brutally attacked by two men, made to suffer unimaginable things, and left to die. He hung there for eighteen hours before being seen by a bicyclist riding by who called 911 and got him help and long-awaited and much needed mercy. Tragically however, he passed away in the hospital from his injuries.

This horrific incident was about power over the powerless and true lack of mercy and I hope we can all agree—no matter our sexual orientation, skin color, or religion—that we all deserve goodness and kindness, justice and mercy. Hearing that this happened shook the nation. People collectively cried and moaned for justice to be done. This cannot be how we treat one another. It just can't. The men who killed him were convicted and are each serving two consecutive life sentences, but my heart strains weak and asks if real justice is truly achievable. What does justice even mean when a man's life is ended at the hand of another? Can a prison sentence really even the score and make it all okay? No, it cannot.

A guilty verdict of the murderers is something, yes, but it does not fill the void left behind. It is a hollow bell's clang and offers no true comfort to the victim's family left forever without their beloved son, grandson, brother. They are left to wade in the deluge of grief, with an empty seat at every family gathering, an endless life sentence of their own to serve without even having committed a crime. How I wish those men chose instead that night to live by Micah's timeless words, "to do what is right to other people, love being kind to others, and live humbly, obeying your God." If they had, this nightmare would have never happened. Oh how I wish it and *so many* similar things would never happen! Why do humans do such things to their fellow man? How are hearts that cruel?

It is when the cracks in the foundations of life widen of how I believe life *should* be and the distance we have fallen seems too vast, that I find a deep need to lean closer to the One who loves mercy, who is all-good and all-kind. I know I can find some peace there in His word when everything seems wrong and my soul is tired, surrounded by so much brokenness and pain. I climb in, nestling down in the soothing and comforting text; "For the Lord is good..."

134

(Psalm 100:5)

And then I remember this truth again: that because we followers of Christ have Him in us, we have the same ability to be good. To be light in the dark places where hope seems buried too deep to broach.

Jesus was publicly called out as good in a profound moment recorded in Scripture: "A certain ruler asked him, 'Good teacher, what must I do to inherit eternal life?'" His response to this person should give us pause. He said, "Why do you call me good?...No one is good—except God alone" (Luke 18:18-19).

Among the many other things He excels at, Jesus is incredibly adept at making us scratch our heads and ponder. Does His response mean that He, in fact, is not God and calling Him that is blasphemy? Or, does He instead mean to call attention to the fact that the man in the story had actually called Him God without understanding the truth of his own words? When we come to a deeper understanding through further study of the Bible, the latter option is the hands-down winner. God was there, covered in flesh and asking the man to pause and think deeper, to walk into the spiritual side of things. Good itself was present in his midst. The inheritance the ruler sought was offered only by the good One just steps away. We all must seek more of God's presence, not only for the much better versions of ourselves, but also for the betterment of others.

Our daughter, Ashley Grace, was born on a cold, gray winter day in January. Every child changes the world's heartbeat and story, and she arrived eager and ready to do her part. She announced her entry with lungs loud and arms flailing, and we had a strong feeling our first child was feisty and full of things to say.

We were not wrong. She was given an extra dose of bold in her blood and justice in her veins. Ashley has lived upright in heart and life even from a young age.

When she was about six years old, she was a kind, funny, spirited little thing. She had then, and still does, an innate desire for goodness and kindness for all. She would see a child being unfairly treated by another at the park and walk right up and defend the defenseless like a mini, dressed-in-pink (head to toe) attorney, fierce and relentless. "Hey!" she would snap. "She had that toy first! Give it back now!" She would stand her ground, argue her case, and win each and every time. Watching her, I could not help but giggle, but also sense feelings of awe welling up in me. She was so strong and sure. My little superhero; determined and brave. Justice had to win.

Still strong in her convictions to this day, Ashley knows who she is and that being kind and good sometimes means calling out others when they are not, and helping someone in need of protection by offering a louder voice than their own. The more I think about this, the more I am undone by it. She is only fourteen years old now, and so rock solid.

Many grown-ups spend countless hours and thousands of dollars on therapy to have what she so naturally owns: agency of who she is and a deep grasp of purpose. I wonder what would have happened if she or someone like her had been present that fateful day when Matthew Shepard was getting beaten and ultimately killed. The outcome could have been different. There would have been someone acting on his behalf, helping him, extending mercy at all cost. Superheroes have no choice but to leap into action; it's in their DNA. Sometimes it just takes one brave, mercy-filled person to change the course of history, for one single family and for the larger, woven-together human family.

I am now asking the hard question of, "Am I willing to be more courageous, driven by goodness and kindness, to birth needed change?" We normal humans gravitate to the superhero types because they seem above the rest of us in their strength, ability, and sense of higher purpose. They fill us with hope for a better world just because they are in it. Can't each of us do such similar good things if we make the words of Micah true for our everyday lives? If we "do what is right to other people, love being kind to others, and live humbly, obeying [our] God."

We will end this chapter with a prayer, given by the Apostle Paul. Let us all remember its wisdom and truth going into each day, with each person we encounter.

And this is my prayer: that your love may abound more and more in knowledge and depth of insight, so that you may be able to discern what is best and may be pure and blameless for the day of Christ, filled with the fruit of righteousness that comes through Jesus Christ—to the glory and praise of God. (Phil. 1:9–11)

We are to do unto others as Christ does for us—be good, be kind, be love in the world no matter the person, place, situation or circumstance. This is our charge as human soldiers. This is our battle cry. Our King has spoken; now we march. Good is possible because God is here. Good is real in us because God is in us. Really! The world changes when we act, for better or worse, so let's all choose better.

CHOOSING... Gentleness: Breaking Through the Chrysalis

Oh! That gentleness! How far more potent it is
than force!

—Charlotte Bronte

I love watching butterflies float and flutter about, their wings laced and delicate, soft and beautiful. Their gentle, unassuming way keeps my gaze, and I admire the innate quality of calm they possess. I really wish I were more like that. Admittedly, I can often be much more bulldozer than butterfly. Too loud, too opinionated, and a bit too brash, I can push and shove my emotional elbows and shoulders when I want to get my point across and want my own way. Speaking before thinking is one of my unspiritual gifts I am afraid and it is not long after I exercise it that I regret my lack of gentleness in my approach to situations and people. Let's just say, if putting your foot in your mouth were a real thing, I would have had to taste the painted toes more than I'd like to admit.

I so desire to be less trumpet more flute. More like a lilting harp than a crashing cymbal. It is well established that opposites attract,

138

and I tend to be very attracted to the gentle people in my midst. They pull me in with their constantly calm, low-lit lantern disposition, soft candle glow to my three-alarm fire. I long to learn this way of being and am feeling a deep-seated thirst for it, desperation even, for the peace and refreshment it offers.

My family and some of our friends started making meals for the homeless a few years back. It began soon after my dad, who had a heart for the needy, passed away. I felt a strong calling to do a ministry for the hungry people living on the streets, and God confirmed the mission and provided in ways that constantly amazed.

It began with twenty meals a week, soon growing to forty. We lovingly filled brown bags with a fresh ham or turkey, cheddar cheese, and lettuce sandwich on wheat bread; a bag of chips; fruit; a homemade cookie or brownie; and a bottle of water each. Our rule was, if we would not genuinely enjoy eating it ourselves, we were not going to serve it to others.

We also put in Scripture verses, reminding the recipients how much God loved them and how important they were; valued and purpose filled. The people were very thankful to receive the meals, sometimes because it was the only food they'd had to eat for days or because it meant they would not have to stand in line for a lunch at the local homeless shelter, which often took hours.

After doing this month after month, halfway through the second year, I noticed one food preparation morning that something had changed in me. My attitude had shifted downward from the high of feeling joyful and Spirit-led about serving God and others to suddenly feeling like the meal ministry was just another to-do list item, another precious-time-sucking task.

Life that week in particular was full and packed tight with not much breathing room left in the week. I had meetings to prepare for and attend and long-overdue floors in my house to clean. I really wanted to have the right motives; to be generous to others with a meek and humble attitude, but my schedule was squeezing me, and my nerves were tense. The jagged and sharp nails of ugly thoughts about rushing through and getting it over with quickly began to dig in, and thankfully I took notice and stopped them quickly, asking God for help. I pleaded, "Lord, please help me to slow down and really connect with the people You have asked me to serve. Let me have eyes to see them as You do and stay in Your gentle spirit. Amen."

After passing out most of the food, I still had not really felt pressed to slow down much and was thinking that maybe God would rather have my floors a bit cleaner after all. Of course, clean hearts are what matter to Him, not vacuumed up floors, so He immediately put a needed hook in me and led me onward. In His glorious and precise way, He showed me His intentions for my time that day, directing my eyes and slowing my steps. He led me to His purpose and waited for me to be faithful to what I had prayed just sixty minutes earlier and seemed to have quickly forgotten.

I was pulling my car away from the curb after passing out all but one of the lunches and noticed a man sitting alone, leaning up against a building on the other side of the street. I pulled back over and parked, grabbed that last meal, and walked over to him. I said my typical thing: "Hi, friend. Are you hungry?" The man looked up at me, his water-blue eyes meeting my hazel, nodded, and happily took the bag. I asked him something, random chitchat, not sure what exactly, and as I did, he investigated the bag's contents and pulled out the sandwich in its Ziploc bag. "Oh, I only have one arm that works," he said.

Looking closer, quieting and lowering myself, listening in between the lines of his comment, I realized he would be unable to open the sandwich bag without a lot of struggle. I offered to help him, and we talked a bit more. He ate a bite and soon after pulled out the bottle of water. I asked, "Can I open that for you?" He said, "Would you? Please." I did, and he once again thanked me. This went on for his entire meal—the gratitude, the eating, the offering, the gratitude, the conversation; sacred circle turning.

We talked, told our stories, and laughed for almost forty-five minutes. The deliberate, God's-hand slowing of my pace, a gentle spirit entering me and changing me, made possible the deeper connection and allowed space for the tender treasure hunt that led to my discovering some of the gems of this man's unique and beautiful life.

I discovered his name was J.C. (John Christopher) and it was his birthday. That day, the day I slowed down, he turned a bit older and I a bit wiser and meeker. It may have been his birthday, but I received the gift of a washing of my soul in gentleness. I am certain it's a day that will stay in my memory forever.

I found out that J.C. had a son who would be visiting him later that day at this crude street corner spot to celebrate. I was told of his time in army service to our nation too. That is how his arm became limp and useless, except as a reminder to him of things he would rather forget.

I realized he was funny right away when I asked what his name was and he said, "My name's J.C., but my friends call me O.G.—

Old Guy." He peered over at me, giggling with a smile in his eyes, his laugh lines bouncing up and down on his face. I also realized that he was a special, gentle, and truly lovely human being who most people would never get to know. Most would pass him by as I would have if God had not shaken my day up by arranging this unforeseen lunch date in a specific answer to prayer.

It was not lost on me that his initials matched my Lord's—J.C., Jesus Christ, the very One I desire most to mirror in thought, word, and deed, including gentleness. The Bible says that we are to not neglect helping others but make gentle, hospitable service a rhythm in our lives, not only because it is good for us and those we help, but also because it is where unseen miracles occur: "Do not forget to show hospitality to strangers, for by so doing some people have shown hospitality to angels without knowing it" (Heb. 13:2).

Sometimes I wonder if J.C. was indeed a hidden angel wrapped in aged, wrinkled skin. If I had remained in my typical state of moving too quickly, bulldozing through, forgetting what this life holds in moments of being gentle and slow, I would have missed out on the blessing this meek stranger offered me. In him, I found connection with another one of God's children and the reminder that God really does hear us and answer us, down to the small, intricate details when we pray. He also reminded me that that nobody God places in our path is accidental or generic. All are purpose-filled encounters, and we must take notice or else miss the miracles.

This is a lesson we learned many times during the ministry of feeding others. We witnessed so many miracles that would have been missed, could have been easily, if the hurry took precedence over the holy. We offered food and kindness, and the ones we

142

served blessed us right back in double portion—God's economy laid out open. By God's system, the meek and gentle gain, the proud and gruff lose. We were given riches money cannot buy, inheriting the goodness of the earth in the transaction (Matt. 5:5).

I have some very godly women in my life who seem to drink gentleness for breakfast. Like a supernatural protein shake, it stays with them all day, keeping them nourished and steady. They have been given an amazing ability to remain peace-filled, it seems, morning till night. Nothing jars or breaks them. I admire them more than the powerful, the wealthy, and the outwardly beautiful. These gentle warrior women have something that the world cannot touch: a deep strength that settles, allowing them to reflect God in the places and situations that make most of us snap and lose it. Like an invisible anchor in the most turbulent of seas, they plant firm to the Rock that never fails them, and in doing so, they can hold emotions in check and hold on to peace.

I am finding, finally, that this is possible even for me. Even for someone whose go-to emotions are fear, stress, and panic when something goes awry. These emotions are bruised and mealy fruit—bad in the mind and mouth, worse in the heart. They fill my life's basket with the bitter, crowding out the better and hindering the holy.

But, when I bring my wayward heart back to ground zero, stripped down and cleaned out, I again remember what I need to do. Toss out the bad, keep the good. Allow the gentle in me to flourish, pushing out the hard, stony dirt, making way for soft grass and the flowering buds. What I seek most: Metamorphosis in Christ. Transformation from hard to soft, bulldozer becoming butterfly.

If I want to do better, and I do, I must offer to others what Jesus offers to me: a gentle grace and eyes that see deeper. I must see deeper in the grocery store when the line is long, and my temper's wick is burning short. In the morning, when the coffee pot cracks and spills, creating the day's first mess and frustrated groans. And in traffic when someone in front is slowing down for no apparent reason, making me late and grouchy.

I begin rearing up, ready for a fight then... God taps my shoulder, asking better of me. He requires that I go lower and lower yet, into the humility and gentleness-filled place where He waits and wants me to find my grounding in Him alone.

We are told to always stay gentle, because there is always a special guest present: "Let your gentleness be evident to all. The Lord is near" (Phil. 4:5). This scripture should remind all of us that gentleness is to be outwardly worn, not tucked away in the folds of our hearts. When something is evident, it is obvious, like a large, conspicuous flower worn in the hair. Those who possess gentleness wear it like this, always seeming to not be rushed or easily upset or pushy. They live their lives like a cool glass of water offered to the overheated, parched types like me. They are a welcome gift.

As is a running theme in this book, this is much easier said than done on so many occasions, especially for types like me. But we still must try our best to do better in this important area of our spiritual growth because Jesus is in our midst, and He cares about it, so we should too.

At my grandmother's wake, I shared a quote often attributed to Maya Angelou that summed up the precious way my grandma lived so many of her own moments: "People will forget what you said, people will forget what you did, but people will never forget how you made them feel." I will never forget the way J.C.'s gentle kindness made me feel that day, like a lost longtime friend being welcomed into his company. I was lost, true. But I found the better part of me that day. J.C. made me want to continue being softer long after our clandestine meeting; he put a desire for his same meek spirit in me.

I do not want to keep missing the miracles waiting for me in this life. I don't want to run over the sacred moments without the reverence they deserve. I know God was there with J.C. and me that day. He certainly made me slow down and take it all in. I got to savor the moment instead of missing it because I listened to and followed Christ's lead. I will try hard to keep rejecting my naturally overbearing ways and instead choose what is better: walking tenderly and slower, staying more calm with the people put in my path, holding on to God's perfectly leading hand.

God asks that we remove our dusty, dirty items that cover our hearts and strip down to the clean and pure to be ready to embrace all that He desires to bring into our lives. He offers many holy opportunities to us; it is simply our job to not overlook or overrun them. The opportunity is just around the bend if we slow down and decide to walk in gentleness.

Thanks, J.C., for helping me do better. Thanks Jesus Christ, my gentle King, for the very same.

CHOOSING... To Daily Clean House

Look into your own heart because who looks outside,
dreams, but who looks inside awakes.

—Jane Austen

We are at this book's end, but not the end of our journey. This making better choices thing is a daily decision we all must make; a revolutionary movement for our souls, an awakening. If we really want to keep ourselves on this higher road, we must make choosing better an intentional and ongoing act, offered up choice by choice and fused with the Holy Spirit's help. We cannot do this in His absence; it is not possible.

I sure wish we could order up "Doing Better" on Amazon with free, expedited shipping and a lifetime warranty in case it ruptures and rips apart. I can imagine the advertisement: "Doing Better: A quick, thoughtless, and simple way to a full life, good choices, and a healed spirit, for today's low price of only $19.99!" Unfortunately, we cannot order with a credit card a full and fulfilled life, because it is not that easy. And besides, the world cannot provide it no matter how much we wish it could. No, to change long-worn patterns of behavior takes serious effort on our part and the true desire for real change at the soul's deepest levels, striving for what is higher, seeking God and His way to way better and abundant life.

It includes daily, sometimes moment-by-moment restraint, involving some failing, some falling, and a lot of getting back up again. This is an everyday all-in effort that we put forth while staying close to Christ for strength to keep going. God does not expect perfection, but He does expect our persistent participation in our own story, He is the Author, but we are not to be idle bystanders. That is part of the wonder of inhabiting space down here—we actually play an important role. He, of course, has the power and might to force anything He wants from us, but then we would learn nothing and not come to understand the secret He has revealed: God is our friend and Father, the lover of our souls, not our puppet master.

Loving Him and loving others is the undergirding and the meaning of our lives. Simply put, but not simply lived. Like any strong bridge that holds weight, our lives must be intentionally structured and designed if we are to withstand what this world brings or throws, high winds and all.

Once we choose God as the guide for our daily attitude and actions and try to live by His example and encouragement, the stone gets rolled away from the heart and God beckons us to emerge brand new. As He said to Lazarus in John 11, all those years ago, He also says to us: "Come out!" (v. 43). The stench and filth of the burial clothes once bound tight, holding us in bondage to hurt, disappointment, and shame are uncoiled and we are set free.

Resurrection, or the invitation to life anew, is available to us all. It is only a choice away. Choosing to be more kind, loving, patient, grateful, and so on is what steeps our days and relationships in goodness—in other words, God Himself. He offers full restoration and renewal if we only will believe. If we stop long enough to seek and find, then our life transformation can begin. Talk about an extreme makeover!

Imagine that you are suddenly dropped into the middle of a fully hoarded-in house. There are books, boxes, food wrappers, toys, tools, containers missing their lids, and everything else you can imagine filling the rooms up to the ceiling. It is hard to walk, let alone breathe. You are disoriented and seemingly trapped with no visible exit.

Then, up the porch steps walks a large, experienced cleaning crew. They knock on the door, offering a free, no-strings-attached spotless cleansing of the home. Relieved, you invite them in. Within a relatively short amount of time, the entire home is sparkling and fresh. The stains are wiped away and the carpet looks brand new. Finally, able to move freely and breathe again, with the weight of the crushing hoard removed, you are overwhelmed with the gift you have just received: A brand new start.

This is what Christ offers us. Now that the engulfing clutter is removed, it is our daily job, by choosing well, to make sure the trash is not allowed to pile up and take over once again. We must keep the house of our heart and mind clean.

Let's remember and heed the advice once again of the Apostle Paul. He says,

Finally, brothers and sisters, whatever is true, whatever is noble, whatever is right, whatever is pure, whatever is lovely, whatever is admirable—if anything is excellent or praiseworthy—think about such things. Whatever you have learned or received or heard from me, or seen in me—put it into practice. And the God of peace will be with you. (Phil. 4:8–9)

Did you catch that promise at the end? If we put God's Word into practice, daily-moment and daily-grind practice, we will be with "the God of peace." What an extraordinary reward! We must remain vigilant to refuse the things that will make us and those around us miserable, choose clarity over clutter and cleanliness over carelessness. Choosing the pure, lovely, excellent, and praiseworthy will give us our hearts' aching desire: The Prince of Peace with us, God with us (Immanuel).

Since earnestly beginning this walk of holding tighter to God's hand, intentionally praying for His help and forgiveness when I falter, and daily studying Scripture, He has done a great, cleansing work in my life. Like past visitors returning to a once hoarded-in home, people now reenter my life relieved and surprised by my renewed presence. They are more comfortable and less on guard knowing I will not do or say something that will crash down on them, causing pain and hurt feelings. They stay and rest easy knowing they are safe here in my company.

Once we have had a whole life makeover and the useless garbage is cleared out, we look different and act differently, changed for the better. Don't our dear loved ones deserve this? Or the countless others we interact with daily—don't they? What about us? Don't we deserve this better way?

The answer, of course, is yes. We do because our good God created us for better, indeed His absolute best. So, going forward, are you with me? Are you ready?

Choose Christ and His priceless offer of complete life

resurrection right here and now and for eternity. You will not regret it, I promise. Promises are hard to make and keep, but this is one I am deeply confident of. In fact, I would bet my life on it. Choosing better will change your life in unimaginable ways. It did mine and still does each and every day.

Thank You, Lord. I could not have done it without You and still cannot. I will keep choosing You and therefore, choosing *better*.

Notes

1. Shauna Niequist, *Present Over Perfect* (Grand Rapids, MI: Zondervan, 2016).

2. *Merriam-Webster.com*, s.v. "Trust," accessed October 28, 2020, https://www.merriam-webster.com/dictionary/trust

3. James Strong, *Strong's Exhaustive Concordance* (Peabody, MA: Hendrickson Publishers, 2007).

4. Luther Ingram, "(If Loving You Is Wrong) I Don't Want to Be Right," Koko, April 1972.

5. Lysa Terkeurst, *It's Not Supposed to Be this Way* (Nashville, TN: Thomas Nelson, 2018).

6. Lysa Terkeurst, *It's Not Supposed to Be this Way*.

7. Johann Hari, "Everything You Know About Addiction Is Wrong," filmed June 2015 in London, TED video, https://www.ted.com/talks/johann_hari_everything_you_think _you_know_about_addiction_is_wrong.

8. Nathaniel Scharping, "Earth May Be a 1-in-700-Quintillion Kind of Place," *Discover Magazine*, February 22, 2016, https://www.discovermagazine.com/the-sciences/earth-may-be-a-1-in-700-quintillion-kind-of-place.

9. Don Batten, "Cheating with Chance," *Creation*, March 1995, pp. 14-15, https://creation.com/cheating-with-chance.

10. Michael Patrick Shiels, "The Truth of What It Is Like to Be Crucified," *Forbes*, March 25, 2015, https://www.forbes.com/sites/michaelshiels/2016/03/25/the-truth-of-what-it-is-like-to-be-crucified/#7f830c921e2f.

11. Lin-Manuel Miranda, Phillipa Soo, and Renee Elise Goldsberry, "It's Quiet Uptown," Warner Chappell Music, Inc, 2015.

12. Martin Luther King Jr. (speech, Montgomery, AL, 1957).

13. Joseph H. Thayer, *Thayer's Greek-English Lexicon of the New Testament* (Peabody, MA: Hendrickson Publishers, 1995).

Thank you so much for buying and reading my book! I am honored.

Please stay in touch with me by visiting and subscribing to my blog: www.choosingbetterdaily.com

Also, please leave a review on the site where you purchased this book – I would be incredibly grateful. God bless you friend!

Yours Truly – Jen Usselman

Made in the USA
Monee, IL
15 December 2020

53557899R00095